Thomas Cogswell Upham

**Christ in the Soul**

Thomas Cogswell Upham

**Christ in the Soul**

ISBN/EAN: 9783337336660

Printed in Europe, USA, Canada, Australia, Japan

Cover: Foto ©Lupo / pixelio.de

More available books at **www.hansebooks.com**

# CHRIST IN THE SOUL;

OR,

ILLUSTRATIONS OF SOME OF THE PRINCIPLES AND EXPERIENCES WHICH CHARACTERIZE CHRIST'S SPIRITUAL OR INWARD COMING AND INDWELLING.

BY

## THOMAS C. UPHAM,

AUTHOR OF
"A SYSTEM OF MENTAL PHILOSOPHY;" "THE MANUAL OF PEACE;" "THE LIFE OF FAITH;" "DIVINE UNION;" &c.

"The kingdom of God is within you."—LUKE xvii. 21.

NEW YORK:
WARREN, BROUGHTON & WYMAN,
13 BIBLE HOUSE.
1872.

# PREFACE.

"CHRIST IN THE SOUL." is a form of expression which is often employed to indicate the fact of the existence, or at least of the possibility of the existence, in the human soul, of pure, holy, Christ-like dispositions. It indicates something more than forgiveness, which is a work done *for* us, rather than something done *in* us. It is not enough, as a portion of our personal Christian history, to know what it is to have our transgressions blotted out,—in other words, to experience the pardon of past delinquencies and sins. There is something more. It is necessary, beyond and above this, to become the subjects also, by inward personal experience, of what may properly be expected as the fruits of forgiveness,—such as meekness, purity, a disposition to forgive, long-suffering, love, and of any and all other graces which shone conspicuously in the life of Christ.

The existence of such Christ-like dispositions, to the extent of essentially reproducing Christ's life upon the earth, is the great problem, and, I trust I may say, is destined to be the great reality, of the future. If there is any foundation for the long cherished anticipations of the Christian world, that there is to be at last a truly millennial period, in which the sins and evils that now exist shall wholly or in a great degree disappear, it must be by the more general incarnation of those holy principles which dwelt in the divine "Son of Man." Believing, as many inquiring persons fully do, that, amid much sin and no small degree of perplexity and tribulation, the world is entering upon a new and better spiritual era, in which righteousness shall ultimately be the rule, and the opposite of righteousness the exception, is it too much to say that it is the part of wisdom to place ourselves in all possible readiness for this great realization.

It is the object of the present volume, by a method somewhat novel, to encourage and aid in this great and essential work;—in other words, to recognize and vindicate a positive heart religion, which shall add to the fact of outward forgiveness the not less important fact of spiritual indwelling and possession. The object is essentially the same with that which I have had in view in some other works already known in some degree to the public, such as The Interior Life, The Life of Faith, Divine Union, and The Biographical Sketches of Madame Guyon and Fénelon. It is to be hoped that the present attempt, in a different form, but which may possibly possess for some minds a degree of interest which they might not find in works of a different kind, may be the means of contributing something to this desirable result. No man ought to regard himself as having secured the great ends of his being until he can speak of those sanctifying results, which are the evidences, or rather the realizations, of Christ or the Christ-life dwelling within.

NEW YORK, *Jan.* 1872.        THOMAS C. UPHAM.

# CONTENTS.

|  | PAGE |
|---|---|
| Christ Within | 13 |
| The Living Temple | 14 |
| Consecration | 15 |
| Sought and Found | 15 |
| The Mystery of the Kingdom | 16 |
| Death to Self | 17 |
| Give All and Take All | 18 |
| Christ in the Soul | 19 |
| Partial and Universal Love | 20 |
| God is Love | 20 |
| Oneness of Life | 21 |
| The Life Power of the Blood | 22 |
| The Measurement of Love | 23 |
| Union with God | 24 |
| Love and Grief | 24 |
| Heaven Within Us | 25 |
| The Sceptre of Love | 26 |
| Leaving all with God | 27 |
| Holiness and Knowledge | 27 |
| Cheerfulness | 28 |
| Compassion | 29 |
| Not Alone | 30 |
| Acceptance of Trials | 31 |
| The Great Resting-place | 32 |
| The Inward and Outward Christ | 33 |

|   |   |
|---|---|
| | PAGE |
| Do Right | 34 |
| Love of the Cross | 35 |
| Let God Answer | 36 |
| On Right Being | 37 |
| Silence under Trials | 38 |
| Good for Evil | 39 |
| The Heavenly Sculptor | 39 |
| The Joys of Penitence | 40 |
| No Separation | 41 |
| The Living Fountain | 42 |
| Resignation | 42 |
| Good Planting | 43 |
| Eternity of Love | 44 |
| Prepare the Inward Temple | 45 |
| Unseen but Seen, | 45 |
| Food for the Soul | 46 |
| Something Left | 47 |
| Waiting | 47 |
| Christ in Man | 48 |
| All Things Equal | 49 |
| Waiting and Guidance | 49 |
| Heavenly Teaching | 50 |
| The World's Light | 51 |
| Help in Sorrow | 51 |
| Judge not | 52 |
| All for the Best | 53 |
| The Promise of the Lord | 54 |
| The Inward Light | 54 |
| Prayer for a Fellow-Sinner | 55 |
| The Christian Soldier | 56 |
| On Going to Heaven alone | 57 |
| The Guidance of Love | 58 |
| Sent of God | 58 |
| The Fire of Love | 59 |
| The Drop and the Ocean | 60 |
| Christ the Way | 61 |
| God's Inward Teaching | 62 |
| God's Glory in His Saints | 62 |
| The Conqueror | 36 |

|   | PAGE. |
|---|---|
| The Joys of the Good | 64 |
| Living by the Moment | 65 |
| Faith in God | 65 |
| Divine Guidance | 66 |
| Keeping Time | 67 |
| The Distant Near | 68 |
| Death of the Me | 68 |
| God in the Darkness | 69 |
| Anticipations | 70 |
| The Hour of Prayer | 71 |
| The Inward Burning | 71 |
| Going Home | 72 |
| The Fruits of Suffering | 73 |
| God and Nothing | 74 |
| Love and Justice | 74 |
| Divine Protection | 75 |
| The Inward Christ | 76 |
| Forgiveness | 77 |
| Follow Jesus | 77 |
| Not Forgotten | 78 |
| Supremacy of Love | 79 |
| Enriched by Giving | 80 |
| Holy Love | 80 |
| Perseverance of Love | 81 |
| Love and the Rod | 82 |
| Rejoicing in Sorrow | 83 |
| A Prayer | 83 |
| The Younger Brotherhood | 84 |
| A Morning Prayer | 85 |
| The Soul and the Sun | 86 |
| Oh, do not Blame Me | 86 |
| Love's Reward | 87 |
| The Good of Sorrows | 88 |
| Leaving the Prison | 89 |
| The Now | 89 |
| Unity of Hearts | 90 |
| Dying Triumphs | 91 |
| Looking to God | 92 |
| Receiving and Giving | 92 |

|   |   |
|---|---|
| The Power of Faith | 93 |
| Christian Benevolence | 94 |
| Love the Soul's Deliverer | 94 |
| Peace and Inspiration | 95 |
| Stand Still | 96 |
| Living by Giving | 97 |
| God's Temple | 98 |
| Work To-Day | 98 |
| Silence | 99 |
| Happy Christians | 100 |
| Christ's Faithfulness | 100 |
| The First and Second Birth | 101 |
| Good for Evil | 102 |
| The Divine Pathway | 103 |
| The New Temple | 103 |
| The Trials of Love | 104 |
| The Joys of Song | 105 |
| Heavenly Light | 106 |
| Following Christ | 106 |
| Gratitude | 107 |
| Change and Permanency | 108 |
| Farewell | 109 |
| Obedience | 109 |
| The Multitude of Slain | 110 |
| Continual Prayer | 111 |
| Sin and Sickness | 112 |
| Christ and Love | 112 |
| I shall yet Praise Him | 113 |
| Meekness of Spirit | 114 |
| Fruits of Love | 114 |
| A Prayer for Love | 115 |
| Riches of Love | 116 |
| Christ in the Soul | 116 |
| Let God Guide | 117 |
| Love the Food of the Soul | 118 |
| Love and Heaven | 118 |
| The Source of Happiness in the Soul | 119 |
| Divine Truth | 120 |
| The Calmer of the Storm | 120 |

|                                       | PAGE |
|---------------------------------------|------|
| Remember thy Calling                  | 121  |
| Divine Strength                       | 122  |
| The Soul's Necessity                  | 122  |
| Faith in Troubles                     | 123  |
| Fulfilment                            | 124  |
| Mystery of the New Birth              | 125  |
| The Heart Searcher                    | 125  |
| A Prayer for Guidance                 | 126  |
| A Prayer for Holiness                 | 127  |
| The New Birth                         | 127  |
| Unity of Life                         | 128  |
| Good Fruits                           | 129  |
| Good in Suffering                     | 129  |
| 'Tis Done                             | 130  |
| Look to Jesus                         | 131  |
| The Power of Love                     | 131  |
| Faith                                 | 132  |
| Death to Self, and Life in God        | 133  |
| He Standeth at the Door               | 134  |
| Despise not the Beginnings            | 135  |
| Meaning of Sorrows                    | 135  |
| The Life of Self                      | 136  |
| Rejoicing in God                      | 137  |
| The Servant and the Son               | 137  |
| Patience                              | 138  |
| All Surrendered and all Gained        | 139  |
| The Way of Bliss                      | 140  |
| The Outward and the Inward            | 140  |
| Follow God                            | 141  |
| Hope On                               | 142  |
| Christ and Love                       | 143  |
| Celestial Visits                      | 143  |
| Help in Christ                        | 144  |
| Past Afflictions                      | 145  |
| Consolation                           | 146  |
| Man the Temple of God                 | 146  |
| One Thing Left                        | 147  |
| The Safe Pilot                        | 148  |
| God Loved in His Creatures            | 149  |

|                                                    | PAGE |
|----------------------------------------------------|------|
| Christ Revealed through His Followers              | 149  |
| Throw off Worldliness                              | 150  |
| The Secret Sign                                    | 151  |
| Triumph in Death                                   | 152  |
| Remembrance in Prayer                              | 153  |
| The Universal Man                                  | 154  |
| Waiting in Faith                                   | 154  |
| The Battle Going On                                | 155  |
| Something to Do                                    | 651  |
| Lines from the Ocean on a Son Lost at Sea          | 157  |
| Christ the Source of Immortal Life                 | 158  |
| The Flower in the Desert                           | 159  |
| The Maiden Fish-Tamer                              | 161  |
| The Star that Shines upon the Heart                | 162  |
| The Sacred Land                                    | 163  |
| God with us in Solitude                            | 164  |
| The Victory of the Cross                           | 166  |
| Resignation and Triumph in Affliction              | 167  |
| The True Rest                                      | 168  |
| God the Source of Love                             | 169  |
| Resource in Temptation                             | 169  |
| Sorrow the Nurse of Love                           | 170  |
| God's Faithfulness                                 | 171  |
| Quietness of Spirit Reflected in the Life          | 172  |
| The Mystic Dove                                    | 173  |

# CHRIST IN THE SOUL.

# CHRIST IN THE SOUL.

### 1.

#### CHRIST WITHIN.

Why would'st thou teach my soul to rise,
And seek for Jesus in the skies?
    Is He so far apart?
Are skies a better dwelling-place
Than man's celestial heart and face,
Made pure and bright with heavenly grace?
    Oh, find Him in thy heart.

Why would'st thou teach my thirsty soul
To wait till death shall make it whole?
    Is Christ so far away?
Oh, no! I see Him now and near;
In my own beating heart I hear
His throbbing life, His voice of cheer;
    He turns my night to day.

Then cease thy looking here and there,
And first of all thy heart prepare,
   By purity from sin;
And then, lit up with heaven's bright glow,
Thy soul of truth and love shall know,
That heaven above is heaven below,
   And Christ is found within.

---

## II.

### THE LIVING TEMPLE.

The Temple once, which brightly shone
   On proud Moriah's rocky brow;
Not there doth God erect His throne,
   And build His place of beauty now.

The sunbeam of the orient day
   Saw nought on earth more bright and fair;
But desolation swept away,
   And left no form of glory there.

But God, who rear'd that chisel'd stone,
   Now builds upon a higher plan;
And rears the columns of His throne,
   His temple in the heart of man.

Oh man, Oh woman! know it well,
   Nor seek elsewhere His place to find,
That God doth in the Temple dwell,
   *The temple of the holy mind.*

## III.

### CONSECRATION.

'Tis done. The "great transaction's past,"
    And I, who call'd myself my own,
Rejecting pride and self, at last
    Belong to God, and God alone.

Dear, Infinite, Eternal Mind!
    Father and Motherhood in one,
May Thy great Life, with mine combin'd,
    Make me a true, a living son.

May all of heart and life be brought
    Within Thine Infinite control;
Be Thou the source of every thought;
    Be Thou the life-spring of the soul.

---

## IV.

### SOUGHT AND FOUND.

Oh Christ! I used to say,
    Help me to come to Thee;
But can I say it now,
    When Christ hath come to me?

Dear Presence in my soul,
    Where thou dost find Thy rest!
Why seek Thee in the skies,
    When dwelling in my breast?

The mother seeks her child,
    When wayward it doth roam;
But seeking hath no place,
    When it is safe at home.

His voice is on my lips;
    His tear bedews mine eye;
His home is in my soul;
    He cannot be more nigh.

Oh no! He is not now,
    A Christ that dwells apart;
But, near as life with life,
    He dwells within my heart.

---

## V.

### THE MYSTERY OF THE KINGDOM.

The mystery of the kingdom lies
    In this, that Christ "*hath died for me;*"
But see, in that great sacrifice,
    The other truth, "*I die for Thee.*"

The life, on bleeding Calvary given,
    Taught us the way our life to save.
All truth, all good, and God, and heaven,
    Are found in giving all we have.

We give up all, and all resume;
    We die the death, and life is born;
Without the shadows of the tomb,
    There comes no resurrection morn.

Down to the grave then let us haste,
  By toiling, suffering, bleeding, giving;
'Tis only thus our souls can taste
  The risen bliss of heavenly living.

---

## VI.

### DEATH TO SELF.

Look not for a true living strength,
  In the life of the ME and the I,
With nothing to love but its self-hood,
  And fearing to suffer and die.
    As thou seekest the fruit
      From the seed-planted grain,
    Seek life that is living,
      From life that is slain.

Then hasten to give it its death-blow,
  By nailing the I to the Cross;
And thou shalt find infinite treasure,
  In what seemeth nothing but loss;
    For where, if the seed
      Is not laid in the ground,
    Shall the germ of the new
      Resurrection be found.

The soul is the Lord's little garden,
  The I is the seed that is there;
And He watches it, while it is dying,
  And hath joy in the fruits it doth bear.

In the seed that is buried,
  Is hidden the power
Of the life-birth immortal,
  Of fruit and of flower.

'Tis hidden, and yet it is true;
  'Tis mystic, and yet it is plain;
A lesson, which none ever knew,
  But souls that are inwardly slain;
    That God, from thy death,
      By His Spirit shall call
    The life ever-living,
      The life, ALL IN ALL.

---

## VII.

### GIVE ALL AND TAKE ALL.

The kingdoms of the world are thine,
  If thou hast faith *thyself* to lose;
But they who seek the ME and MINE,
  The universal good refuse.

The master of his own desire,
  The victor over selfish claims,
Doth by that DEATH OF SELF aspire
  To universal ends and aims.

He breaks his bars and prison bound;
  And in his free, imperial soul,
Hath boldly reached, and nobly found
  The wide, the bright, the kingly whole.

The gems, in hidden mines that glow,
    The stars, that shine beyond the skies,
The heavens above, the earth below,
    ALL, ALL, are his, to SELF, who dies.

---

## VIII.

### CHRIST IN THE SOUL.

Thou sayest, it shall surely be,
    That Christ, the Lord, shall come again;
And, in His scepter'd majesty,
    His royal state maintain.

'Tis *well*. Already hath He come;
    Already in the holy soul,
He makes His high and scepter'd home,
    And wields supreme control.

Christ in the heart is holy LOVE;
    Nor doth He make a higher claim;
In earth below, in heaven above,
    LOVE is His "hidden name."

He comes; but not to outward view;
    He comes and makes the spirit whole:
He comes, the Beautiful, the True,
    The Love-life of the soul.

## IX.

### PARTIAL AND UNIVERSAL LOVE.

There is a love; a love for *one* ;
   On one alone its blessings fall;
But *heavenly* love is like the sun;
   It throws its golden light on ALL.

The love, which holy heaven imparts,
   To narrow limits unconfin'd,
Extends the sympathy of hearts
   To friends, to foes, to all mankind.

There's nothing which it calls its own;
   In *self* it hath no power to live;
And 'tis by this its life is known,
   That what it hath, *it hath to give.*

Oh holy Love! Oh heavenly Love!
   To hearts of truth and virtue given;
The Love, that lives in hearts above;
   The Love, that makes of earth a heaven.

---

## X.

### GOD IS LOVE.

Men make such idols as they choose,
   And worship low before their throne;
But little know they what they lose,
   In not enthroning LOVE alone.

Before great LOVE the angels bow,
  Moving in radiant, joyful bands;
And Love, controlling here and now,
  Unites our hearts, and joins our hands.

Remember, God himself is LOVE;
  And is there other throne than His,
Who reigns below, who reigns above,
  Supreme in truth, supreme in bliss?

Before celestial Love bow down;
  All selfish deities remove;
Bright as the heavens shall be the crown
  Of those, whose hearts are fill'd with LOVE.

---

## XI.

### ONENESS OF LIFE.

If life on earth, and life in heaven,
  As ancient seers and prophets say,
Is from the same great radiance given,
  And burns with one celestial ray;

If brightness there, and brightness here,
  Is in its central nature one;
And, shining in whatever sphere,
  Is from the same imperial sun;

Oh, then, come down, and fill my heart,
  Great God with Thine own life of love,
So that I may not stand apart
  From the bright life, which shines above.

The secret of the heavens reveal,
  And make its inward glory known,
Till all of thought and heart and will,
  And life itself are made Thine own.

## XII.

### THE LIFE POWER OF THE BLOOD.

He dies, and from His bleeding veins,
The fountain of His life-blood drains
  To cleanse the stains of sins;
And nothing less than that dear tide,
Which flow'd from Jesus' bleeding side,
  Can make us pure within.

But underneath that fountain lies
A fount, unseen by outward eyes,
  Eternal from above;
Of which the blood is but the sign,
Which gives that blood its power divine;
  The deeper fount of LOVE.

LOVE flows beneath the purple flood;
LOVE is the life-power of the blood;
  LOVE, offering to be slain;
'Tis LOVE that to thy heart applies
The emblem of its sacrifice;
  And washes out thy stain.

And wouldst thou learn the heavenly art,
To bear about a holy heart,
   Let kindred love be thine;
The same dear love, which ever flows,
In tears and blood, for others' woes,
   And makes thy life divine.

---

## XIII.

### THE MEASUREMENT OF LOVE.

Go, count the sands that form the earth,
   The drops that make the mighty sea;
Go, count the stars of heavenly birth,
   And tell me what their numbers be,
   And thou shalt know LOVE's mystery.

No measurement hath yet been found,
   No lines or numbers that can keep
The sum of its eternal round,
   The plummet of its endless deep,
   Or heights, to which its glories sweep.

Yes, measure LOVE, when thou canst tell
   The lands where seraphs have not trod,
The heights of heaven, the depths of hell,
   And lay thy finite measuring-rod
   On the infinitude of God.

## XIV.

### UNION WITH GOD.

I pray'd, O God, that I might be,
So fashioned, and so bound to Thee,
With such dear links and bonds of heart,
That I could never stand apart
From time or place, where'er Thou art.

And wilt Thou leave me, Holy One,
When thus to Thee my soul doth run?
Oh no! When God Himself shall die,
And not till then, wilt Thou deny
My constant, struggling, heartfelt cry.

The morning sunbeams are the same
With the great sun from which they came;
And so, in unity divine,
Thou hearest, and dost make me Thine,
And all my Father hath is mine.

---

## XV.

### LOVE AND GRIEF

Love sometimes scales the mountain height,
   In joys and ecstasies sublime;
But oftener takes the downward flight,
   And sheds its tears for woe and crime.
Love and Grief go side by side;
Christ was Love; He bled and died.

Love plucks the flowers of Olivet,
    And plays with daylight's fading sea;
But when that parting sun is set,
    It seeks thy shades, Gethsemane!
Love and Grief go side by side,
Christ was Love; He bled and died.

Gethsemane! Divinely sent,
    Though bitter be its draught of woe,
Is mix'd with Love's dear element,
    And love and tears together flow.
Love and Grief go side by side.
Christ was Love; He bled and died.

---

## XVI.

### HEAVEN WITHIN US.

"*It is time to be thinking of heaven,*"
    So the voice of the teachers doth say;
But the heaven to which they would lead us,
    Is a heaven that is far, far away.

They tell us, that, o'er the dark river,
    We will land on the heavenly shore;
But is it not wiser and better,
    To find that bright Canaan before?

"The kingdom of God is within you,"
    The greatest of Teachers hath said;
And the faithful and loving have found it,
    And enjoy'd it, before they were dead.

The kingdom of God is within you;
　　Let doubtings and sorrows depart.
*The kingdom of God is within you;*
　　It dwells in the sanctified heart.

---

## XVII.

### THE SCEPTRE OF LOVE.

I hold the sceptre in my hand,
　　Which rules the universe of things;
Which rules the ocean, rules the land,
　　And puts to shame the power of kings.

The iron wheels of cruel war,
　　The swords and scimetars of strife!
They see its glories from afar,
　　And bow before its power of life.

Look up! Its lifted light behold;
　　Not fram'd by human power or art;
Not made of wood, or stone, or gold;
　　'Tis LOVE! the sceptre of the heart.

'Tis LOVE! All things shall love obey;
　　All things its high behests fulfill;
It holds the thunders in its sway;
　　It says to stormy seas, "Be still."

My Father smiled, and bade me take,
　　My infant hand, that sceptre fair;
Beneath its power the nations shake,
　　*For God's Omnipotence is there.*

## XVIII.

### LEAVING ALL WITH GOD.

Oh God, Thou knowest what is best,
   And as my weakness cannot see
What things will make my spirit blest,
   *Help me to leave my choice with Thee.*

With flattering lips if power or fame
   Should ask me, that they may be mine,
Aid me against their tempting claim
   To say, I have no choice but Thine.

Weakness is better far than power,
   And poverty than house or land,
If, in their dark and trying hour,
   Thy love shall hold me by the hand.

O let me in Thyself abide;
   In Thee is wealth and power divine.
Rend from my grasp all else beside;
   But let me know, that I AM THINE.

---

## XIX.

### HOLINESS AND KNOWLEDGE.

Wouldst thou the key of knowledge hold,
And with its mighty touch unfold
The secret in its breast that lies,
Of earth's and heaven's mysteries?

Hast thou the sacred, strong desire,
To truth's bright summit to aspire;
And with the aspiration glow,
Which seeks to know, as angels know?

Oh, then, that key of knowledge gain,
By pride, and self, and passion SLAIN;
Oh, then, that height of vision win,
By LIFE to God, and DEATH to sin.

It is pollution of the mind,
Which makes its power of knowledge blind;
'Tis PURITY, which pours the light
Of heavenly vision on the sight.

## XX.

### CHEERFULNESS.

The bird is happy all the day,
   The morning hears his early songs;
The love, that breathes the morning lay,
   To evening's shade the note prolongs.
Never weary, never fearful,
Always singing, always cheerful.

Is man less happy than a bird?
   Has he less power his song to raise?
Why, then, so seldom is he heard
   In the glad notes of joy and praise?
Often weary, often fearful,
Seldom singing, seldom cheerful.

Oh, be a bird, a cheerful bird;
  Thy love like his, as pure and free;
Till all the earth and air is stirred
  With notes of joy and liberty.
Never weary, never fearful,
Always singing, always cheerful.

---

## XXI.

### COMPASSION.

"JUDGE NOT," the heavenly Teacher says,
Judge not, your erring brother's ways;
It is the great, omniscient part
Of God alone, to know the heart.

'Tis God alone the trial knows
Of Him, in error's paths who goes;
The secret, hidden, tempting power,
Which ruled him in the dangerous hour.

And since the wicked deed was done,
'Tis known to God, and God alone;
What bitter sighs, what scalding tears,
Have rued that deed of other years.

Though Priest and Levite pass him by,
Oh, let him have Thy pitying eye;
Thy tender look, Thy heart-felt prayer,
A brother's love, a sister's care.

## XXII.

### NOT ALONE.

I cannot be alone;
  Where'er I go, I find,
Around my steps, the presence thrown
  Of the Eternal Mind.

He lives in all my thoughts;
  His home is in my heart;
There is no loneliness for me;
  I never live apart.

I sometimes go from men,
  Far in the silent woods;
But He is with me even then,
  In shady solitudes.

The fellow of my walks,
  Companion ever nigh,
He fills the solitary place,
  With love and sympathy.

I cannot be alone,
  Where'er I go, I find,
Around my steps, the presence thrown,
  Of the Eternal Mind.

## XXIII.

### ACCEPTANCE OF TRIALS.

'Tis all the same to me;
Sorrow, and strife, and pining want, and pain!
Whate'er it is, it cometh all from Thee,
And 'tis not mine to doubt Thee or complain.

Thou knowest what is best;
And who, oh God, but Thee hath power to know?
'Tis Thine alike with good to make us blest,
And Thine to send affliction's hour of woe.

No questions will I ask.
Do what Thou wilt, my Father and my God!
Be mine the dear and consecrated task,
To bless the loving hand that lifts the rod.

All, all shall please me well;
Since living faith hath made it understood,
That in the shadowy folds of sorrow dwell
The seeds of life and everlasting good.

---

## XXIV.

### INWARD VICTORY.

Smite on! It doth not hurt me now;
　The spear hath lost its edge of pain;
And piercing thorns, that bound my brow,
　No longer leave their bleeding stain.

What once was woe is changed to bliss;
   What once was loss is now my gain;
My sorrow is my happiness;
   My life doth live by being slain.

The birth-pangs of those dreadful years
   Are like the midnight changed to morn;
And daylight shines upon my tears,
   Because the soul's great life is born.

The piercing thorns have changed to flowers;
   The spears have grown to sceptres bright;
And sorrow's dark and sunless hours
   Become eternal days of light.

## XXV.

### THE GREAT RESTING PLACE.

The brooks rush downward to the sea,
   Arising far in cliffs and mountains;
But mingling soon in unity,
   They make great streams from little fountains.

And then the streams, without delay,
   Still to the sea's great bosom tending,
Roll proudly on their winding way,
   At last with ocean's billows blending.

And so, oh God, our souls to Thee,
   Onward and onward, ever going,
(We are the fountains, Thou the sea,)
   To Thy great sea of life are flowing.

Yes! One with God, as Christ is one,
   No longer tost by earth's commotion,
Our little streams, their journey done,
   Shall rest, at last, in God's great ocean.

---

## XXVI.

### THE INWARD AND OUTWARD CHRIST.

The CHRIST WITHIN, by works is known,
In deeds of truth and goodness shown;
The Inward life, He outward lives,
And all He hath, to others gives.

Above all thoughts of coward fear,
He goes where pestilence is near;
When griefs assail, when lov'd ones die,
He cheers the heart, He wipes the eye.

His hand doth ope the prison door;
He feeds the hungry, starving poor;
He loves to heal their wounds, and bind
The broken, penitential mind.

He knows no clime, no sect, no name;
All tribes and sects to Him the same;
The Greek, the Jew, the bond, the free,
Alike receive His sympathy.

## XXVII.

[CHRIST IN THE SOUL, is an expression, embracing all the mental or spiritual elements, which constitute the Christian character. It includes, therefore, the sentiment of rectitude, the soul's law of right, as well as the strictly religious affections.]

### DO RIGHT.

Go BOLDLY ON. Do what is right;
   Ask not for private ease or good;
Let one bright star direct thy sight,
   The polar star of rectitude.

Go boldly on. And though the road
   Thy weary, bleeding feet shall rend,
Angels shall help thee bear thy load,
   And God Himself thy steps attend.

Do RIGHT. And thou hast nought to fear;
   Right hath a power that makes thee strong;
The night is dark, but light is near;
   The grief is short, the joy is long.

Know, in thy dark and troubled day,
   To friends of truth and right are given,
When strifes and toils have pass'd away,
   The sweet rewards and joys of heaven.

## XXVIII.

### LOVE OF THE CROSS.

O Father! Let me bear the Cross,
   Make it my daily food,
Though with it Thou dost send the loss
   Of every other good.

Take house and lands and earthly fame;
   To all I am resigned;
But let me make one earnest claim;
   Leave, leave the Cross behind!

I know it costs me many tears,
   But they are tears of bliss;
And moments there outweigh the years
   Of selfish happiness.

The Cross is Love, to action given;
   Love "seeking not its own;"
But finding truth and peace and heaven,
   In good to others shown.

The Cross doth live in God's great life,
   In Christ's dear heart doth shine;
And how, without its pains and strife
   Shall God and Christ be mine?

## XXIX.

### LET GOD ANSWER.

When wicked men thy patience try,
   With haughty words and threats and blows,
Let *God*, and not *thyself*, reply;
   Thy wants the Father knows.

'Tis He, with kindly presence near,
   Thy words and feelings shall inspire;
Thy foes shall tremble when they hear
   Lips touch'd by heaven's own fire.

The strength of human argument
   And human wit, shall fail to reach
The mighty power, the great intent,
   Of God's interior speech.

LEAVE ALL WITH GOD, and, in the hour
   Of greatest feebleness and need,
Behold the triumph of His power;
   TO GOD ALONE TAKE HEED.

---

## XXX.

### THE NEW BIRTH.

BE BORN AGAIN,
   With birth-right from above;
Thy selfish nature slain;
   Be born of LOVE.

'Tis life from heaven,
    Descending in thy soul;—
'Tis Love's new nature given,
    Which makes thee whole.

Oh, do not rest,
    Till that bright hour shall come,
Which smites thy selfishness
    With final doom.

And, in its place,
    Brings forth the life, new-born
Of truth, and love, and peace,
    Bright as the morn.

---

## XXXI.

### ON RIGHT BEING.

To think, to feel, to act, to BE,
This is life's mighty mystery;
But BEING is the secret spring,
From which the rest their birth-right bring.

The central source, hid deep within,
With Being all our acts begin;
And thought, and sentiment as well,
Within the folds of Being dwell.

'Tis thus the life-power of the soul,
And hath o'er all its acts control;
And as there's truth or falsehood there,
There's truth or falsehood everywhere.

So let the BEING, made divine,
With central truth and glory shine;
And then the stamp and seal of heaven
To feeling, thought, and act are given.

---

## XXXII.

### SILENCE UNDER TRIALS.

When words and acts, untrue, unkind,
   Against thy life, like arrows, fly;
Receive them with a patient mind;
   *Seek no revenge, make no reply.*

Oh holy SILENCE! 'Tis the shield,
   More strong than warrior's twisted mail;
A hidden strength, a might conceal'd,
   Which worldly shafts in vain assail.

He, who is silent in his cause,
   Has left that cause to heavenly arms;
And heaven's eternal aid and laws
   Are swift to ward the threatening harms.

God is our great, protecting Power.
   BE STILL! The great Defender moves;
He watches well the dangerous hour;
   Nor fails to save the child He loves.

## XXXIII.

### GOOD FOR EVIL.

They do not know us. If they did,
    They would not blame and smite us so.
To selfish hearts the light is hid,
    And being blind, they cannot know.

Then let us not with anger burn,
    Resembling thus our cruel foes;
But, when the cheek is smitten, turn
    The other meekly to their blows.

With such forgiving words and deeds,
    We claim the aid of that great Power,
Who knows His trusting people's needs,
    And guards them in their trying hour.

God is thy battle's mighty arm;
    God is thy great, victorious sword.
To him there comes nor fear nor harm,
    Whose confidence is in the Lord.

---

## XXXIV.

### THE HEAVENLY SCULPTOR.

Shrink not from suffering. Each dear blow,
    From which thy smitten spirit bleeds,
Is but a messenger to show
    The renovation which it needs.

The earthly sculptor smites the rock;
    Loud the relentless hammer rings;
And from the rude, unshapen block,
    At length, imprisoned beauty brings.

Thou art that rude, unshapen stone;
    And waitest, till the arm of strife
Shall make its crucifixions known,
    And smite and carve thee into life.

The Heavenly Sculptor works on THEE;
    BE PATIENT. Soon His arm of might,
Shall from thy prison's darkness free,
    And change thee to a form of light.

---

## XXXV.

### THE JOYS OF PENITENCE.

FAREWELL! Thine earthly strife is o'er;
    Thine earthly sorrows past;
Jesus, thy friend, hath gone before;
    And thou art free at last.

No more the solitude and pain;
    No more the bitter tear;
A better land thy soul shall gain,
    Than that, which held thee here.

Earth's children did not understand
    The sorrows of thy heart;
But spirits of the heavenly land
    Shall judge thee as thou art.

A soul that erred, a soul restored,
    A soul that sinned, a soul forgiven;
Dear to the Christ, the loving Lord,
    And safe, at last, in heaven.

## XXXVI.

### NO SEPARATION.

Oh, can I leave Thee! Can I go
    Back to the world that once was nigh?
And so debase me, as to know
    The joys that only bloom to die?

Oh, can I quit celestial good,
    The growth of life's immortal tree,
And feed, instead of Angel's food,
    On earth's poor dust and vanity?

I sought Thee, that my soul might stay
    In endless unity of mind;
And dare not, cannot rend away
    The golden links my heart that bind.

If others blindly choose to roam,
    And find the path of tears and gloom;
Be MINE, in God's great heart, the home,
    Where peace, and joy, and glory bloom.

## XXXVII.

### THE LIVING FOUNTAIN.

I hear the tinkling camel's bell
    Beneath the shade of Ebal's mount,
And man and beast, at Jacob's well,
    Bow down to taste the sacred fount.

Samaria's daughter too doth share
    The draught that earthly thirst can quell;
But who is this that meets her there?
    What voice is this at Jacob's well?

" Ho! ask of *me*, and I will give,
    From my own life, *thy* life's supply;
*I* am the fount! drink, drink and live;
    No more to thirst, no more to die!"

Strange mystic words, but words of heaven;
    And they who drink to-day, as then,
To them shall inward life be given;
    *Their souls shall never thirst again!*

---

## XXXVIII.

### RESIGNATION.

Oh, let the fires of trouble burn;
    Seek not too soon to quench the flame;
In peaceful Resignation learn,
    The better way their wrath to tame.

Resistance, which thy fears inspire,
  Doth not protect, doth not restore;—
'Tis rather fuel for the fire,
  And makes it blaze and burn the more.

But when thy troubled soul accepts
  The furnace of its wasting grief;
A power unseen thy life protects;
  'Tis Christ himself that brings relief.

Oh yes, 'tis Jesus with thee stands;
  The heated fires grow weak and dim;
He shields thee with His outstretch'd hands;
  His ARM IS ROUND THEE. Trust in Him.

---

## XXXIX.

### GOOD PLANTING.

TEAR from thy heart the poisonous weed
  Of *self* and *sin*, that's growing there;
And PLANT, instead, celestial seed;
  And thus eternal fruitage bear.

Not by "the way side" shall it grow;
  Not in a hard and rocky soil;
But where it shall not fail to know
  The cultivator's tears and toil.

Plant in the good and honest heart;
  Not tares, but heaven's celestial grain;
And pray the heavenly Father's art,
  To give the sunshine and the rain.

And from that seed and sacred root,
    The bud and flower thou soon shalt see;
The fragrant bloom, the golden fruit,
    Of Eden's bright, immortal tree.

---

## XL.

### ETERNITY OF LOVE.

Oh Love! The life-power of my heart,
    If all things else should die,
There's one thing, that can never part,
    There's one thing ever nigh.

I look upon the worlds above;
    Their light may all decay;
But there's eternal life in Love;
    Love cannot pass away.

Oh sun, that in thy fading years,
    May cease at last to shine,
Thou canst not whisper to my fears,
    That such a lot is mine.

Oh no! the shining sun may fade,
    And wither like a scroll;
But death is powerless to invade
    The love-light of the soul.

## XLI.

### PREPARE THE INWARD TEMPLE.

He dwelt in Tents in olden time;
    Then built Moriah's gilded shrine;
But *now*, in temples more sublime,
    In HOLY HEARTS, his glories shine.

And if in Christ He first appear'd,
    Dear shrine of beauty, truth, and bliss;
He now appears in temples rear'd
    In other hearts, akin to His.

Oh, cleanse THY SOUL from every sin,
    From every grovelling, worldly care;
And let the mighty Monarch in,
    To build His throne of glory there.

---

## XLII.

### UNSEEN BUT SEEN.

He doth not to our sight appear;
And yet the Christ, the King is here.
He is not seen by outward eye,
And yet we feel and know Him nigh.

In holy hearts He builds His throne;
By holy thoughts His presence known;
And most of all He makes His reign,
Where Love is life, where Self is slain.

Oh Life of love, oh Christ within!
A Life, without the stains of sin;
Unknown, unseen by outward sight,
We see Thee in the soul's clear light.

---

## XLIII.

### FOOD OF THE SOUL.

The hungry, starving soul doth cry,
    Feed me, or I must cease to be;
And let the bread of love supply
    My spirit's great necessity.

*Nor think it strange.* All things of life
    Require their food, their vital air;
And perish on their field of strife,
    If life's supplies are wanting there.

The dews descend on thirsty flowers;
    The heavens send radiance from above;
And so these hungry souls of ours
    Live in the dews and rays of love.

Jesus is Love; the living Bread;
    His own dear life He doth bestow;
And souls, who on that life are fed,
    The pangs of hunger shall not know.

## XLIV.

### SOMETHING LEFT.

Let want and persecution come,
And grief in all its forms of gloom;
Fear not. Thy strength is from above.
Fear not. Thou yet hast power to LOVE.

Let tribulation's evil day
Take friends, and home, and wealth away;
Fear not. Though all things else may part,
They cannot take away the heart.

The power to LOVE doth still remain,
With goods bereft, and prospects slain;
The power to LOVE, which cannot die,
When all things else in ruin lie.

If this is left, not all is gone;
If this is left, march boldly on;
If this is left, thou still art whole;
LOVE is the Heaven of the soul.

---

## XLV.

### WAITING.

'Tis a great lesson which we learn,
   In this our weak and trying state,
To see God's hand at every turn,
   And patiently to wait.

Conceal'd in mysteries sublime,
    When painful months and years are past,
The things, deep hidden for a time,
    Are all revealed at last.

We know them then, but know not now;
    We walk by faith and not by sense;
And cheerfully and humbly bow
    Before Thy Providence.

Oh God, this blessedness impart,
    This foretaste of a heavenly state,
The gift of a believing heart,
    Which patiently can wait.

---

### XLVI.

#### CHRIST IN MAN.

How beautiful the wondrous plan
Of God in Christ, and Christ in man;
Which helps prophetic souls to trace
Bright heaven beneath the human face.

'Tis true, He shines in brook and tree;
But, brighter shines, oh man, in thee.
Oh, dim not with the shades of sin,
The glory, which should gleam within.

In thee doth Jesus walk the earth;
In thee He speaks of heavenly birth;
In thee instructs, in thee rebukes,
With wisdom, not in earthly books.

Look not to heaven's celestial dome;
In holy hearts He makes His home;
And let it be thy thought and care,
To seek, and find, and know Him there.

---

## XLVII.

### ALL THINGS EQUAL.

ALL THINGS ARE EQUAL to the soul,
  That doth no private ends fulfil;
But bends beneath the just control
  Of God, the great, the sovereign Will.

It sees, in all things high and low,
  The presence of a higher care;
And if there's much it doth not know,
  'Tis sure of this, that God is there.

It sees Him in the stormy cloud;
  It sees Him in the smiling sun;
And says, with thoughts and purpose bow'd,
  In light and cloud, "THY WILL BE DONE."

---

## XLVIII.

### WAITING AND GUIDANCE.

WAIT ON THE LORD, to learn the time
  And circumstance of every deed;
He loves to bow His thought sublime
  To those who wait, and feel their need.

He knows the time, He knows the way,
   And He alone can give the light,
Which will not lead our steps astray,
   But teach and guide them in the right.

Oh, then in RECOLLECTION wait,
   In calmness look, till light is given;
And thus thou shalt not miss the straight
   And narrow way that leads to heaven.

---

### XLIX.

#### HEAVENLY TEACHING.

The selfish heart for wisdom looks
In earth's dim leaves and mouldering books;
The holy heart its light doth find
In God's great light and living Mind.

The holy heart, of love compact,
With love in every thought and act,
Doth find, *within*, the Teacher true,
With thoughts and lessons ever new.

The secret whispers, inly heard,
The voice, of the "Eternal Word,"
Surpass in wisdom, far, the reach
Of what poor earthly schoolmen teach.

Oh WISDOM, coming from above,
The eldest born, the child of LOVE,
Be Thou our book, our living page,
To guide us through earth's pilgrimage.

## L.

### THE WORLD'S BRIGHT LIGHT.

Oh Love! Thou art that heavenly fire,
Which burneth up all low desire;
A holy flame, that food doth find,
In loving, blessing all mankind.

With step and majesty divine,
And knowing nought of "ME" and "MINE,"
Thy living breath, thy life's supply,
Is universal sympathy.

Unlike the coursers in the race,
Thou hast no bounds of time and place;
But south and north, and east and west,
Thou seekest all, in all art blest.

Oh Love! Bright heaven is on thy wing;
That heaven o'er all the nations fling;
Scatter its glory near and far,
THE WORLD'S BRIGHT LIGHT AND MORNING STAR.

---

## LI.

### HELP IN SORROW.

Fear not, poor, weary one;
  But struggle bravely yet;
Toil on, until thy task is done,
  Until thy sun is set.

Though many are thy cares,
    And many are thy fears,
The loving Christ thy burden shares,
    And wipes away thy tears.

No distant Christ is He,
    And one that doth not know;
But watches close and constantly,
    The path which thou dost go.

'Tis when thy heart is tried,
    'Tis in thine hour of grief,
He standeth ever at thy side,
    And ever brings relief.

## LII.

### JUDGE NOT.

Oh, do not judge thy fellow man;
    Reproachful epithets forbear;
He hath his place in Heaven's great plan;
    The God, who made, hath placed him there.

He's POOR. But in his rags behold
    A heart of pure and high intent;
And if his form is bent and old,
    It is no cause of merriment.

Perhaps he's EVIL. Let thy prayer
    Implore the God of truth and grace,
That soon his footsteps may repair
    To virtue's bright and better ways.

OH, DO NOT JUDGE HIM. Had'st thou been,
    Cast out like him to pine and die,
Thou too, allur'd and stain'd by sin,
    Hadst needed tears of sympathy.

---

## LIII.

### ALL FOR THE BEST.

We dare not doubt, that all will end
    In what is good, and true, and best;
That all we suffer here will tend
    To make us pure, and wise, and blest.

'Tis true, rebellious thoughts arraign
    The mysteries of God's decree;
But hearts of love will not complain
    Of aught, that hath its source in Thee.

'Tis Thine, to mould us at Thy will,
    Oh God, the artist of the soul;
'Tis ours, to sit, in meekness, still,
    Beneath the blows, that make us whole.

Then smite us here, and smite us there,
    As best Thy Providence shall find;
Afflictions, sent from heaven, repair,
    And mould, and beautify the mind.

## LIV.

### THE PROMISE OF THE LORD.

We thank Thee, Lord, before 'tis done;
    We know Thy promise doth endure;
And battles fought are battles won,
    *Because Thy word is sure.*

Look back, and confirmation see
    In the long history of years;
When God hath uttered his decree,
    No place remains for fears.

There's something brighter than the light
    Of burnish'd spear and gleaming sword;
Gird on the heavenly armor bright,
    The strength of God's great word.

Behold the boasting foemen flee
    With flags and cohorts crush'd and broken;
'Tis God, that gives the victory;
    *The Lord himself hath spoken.*

---

## LV.

### THE INWARD LIGHT.

There was a man; and he was blind;
And yet he said, the Lord is kind;
For, while he takes the outward sight,
He gives me more of inward light;
The inward light, the inward light,
*He gives me more of inward light.*

The outward sight is very dear,
With power to know, and power to cheer;
It visits field and fruit and flower,
And running stream and sunny bower;
But know, that not till that is seal'd,
Is all of inward light reveal'd.

The soul, to outward objects blind,
Opens the eye-lids of the mind;
And to the sun-beams from the sky,
That light its deep, interior eye,
The truths, unseen before, are given,
Which shine like stars, and guide to heaven.

Oh God, the Universal Whole,
Visit the Temple of the soul;
Oh God, the living light within,
Dispel the shades and clouds of sin;
Take, if Thou wilt, the outward sight,
And quench its rays in sunless night,
*But give, oh give the inward light.*

---

## LVI.

### PRAYER FOR A FELLOW SINNER.

Pity, O Lord, the wandering one,
   The outcast of the sons of men;
Against Thyself his deeds were done;
   Wilt Thou not take him back again?

Bend down, and catch his weary sigh,
  And let him in his anguish hear
The footsteps of his Father nigh,
  To break his chain, to wipe his tear.

I too have been a sinner, Lord ;
  I too like him have gone astray,
Forgetful of Thy holy Word,
  And walking in the devious way.

Pity my brother in his wrong ;
  Pity, as Thou hast pitied me ;
And, with Thy tender arm and strong,
  Set the poor bleeding captive free.

---

## LVII.

### THE CHRISTIAN SOLDIER.

The archer's arrow smote me sore,
  Sped by a skilful foeman's hand ;
And, though I bled at every pore,
  The faith within me bade me, STAND.

The MASTER plac'd me ; and He knew,
  His orders were my only law ;
And 'twas not one, when arrows flew,
  That I should cowardly withdraw.

The soldiers in the Christian war,
  With much to do, and much to dare,
Proclaim, in every bleeding scar,
  Their faith in Him, who placed them there.

> Great Chief and Leader of the strife!
>   Thy death has taught us how to die;
> And if with Thee we yield our life,
>   Then death itself is victory.

---

## LVIII.

### ON GOING TO HEAVEN ALONE.

High in the hills the wild bird hath its nest,
  And utters loud its melodies of song;
But vain its music, if no other breast
  Is there to mate it, and its notes prolong.

And so in heaven, think not to dwell alone,
  In cold and hopeless solitude apart;
For heaven is love; and love would leave its throne,
  If at its side there were no other heart.

Then heaven-ward soar, *but carry others there;*
  And learn, that heaven is giving and receiving;
It hath no life, which others do not share;
  Its life doth live by its great art of giving.

Heaven is the heart, to other love-hearts beating;
  'Tis open arms, to arms of fondness rushing;
'Tis songs, with other songs in concert meeting;
  'Tis fountains into other fountains gushing.

## LIX.

### THE GUIDANCE OF LOVE.

If thou wouldst be of heavenly mind,
Thy soul's great light no longer blind,
Then from *thyself* thy soul set free,
And soar in Love's great liberty.

As thou art now, thou dost not know,
Where it is best to stay or go;
But, once from selfish guidance freed,
Shalt learn, where truth and duty lead.

No longer dangers shalt thou fear;
But filled with hope and inward cheer,
Shalt see and shun with open eye
The pitfalls, that before thee lie.

From early youth to weary age,
In all his earthly pilgrimage,
Shall truth and guidance never part
From him, who hath the loving heart.

---

## LX.

### SENT OF GOD.

It was a dark, untravell'd road,
  In which my steps were call'd to go;
The path of many a heavy load,
  And where it led, I did not know.

A weary road with rivers high;
  Wild beasts were standing on the rocks;
And clouds came drifting through the sky,
  Fill'd deep with fires and thunder shocks.

But through the clouds, and through the flame,
  And foaming floods, as on I went,
A voice of hope and cheering came,
  "*Fear not to go, where God hath sent.*"

That voice is ringing in my ears;
  Let mountains rise, let oceans flow;
It matters not. Away with fears.
  IF GOD DOTH SEND ME, LET ME GO.

---

## LXI.

### THE FIRE OF LOVE.

If thou would'st slay thy wrong desire,
  Thy hate and ills of every kind,
Plunge them in LOVE's consuming fire;
  Love is the furnace of the mind.

Whate'er their kind, degree, or name,
  The evils, which thy heart enthral,
It matters not, LOVE's mighty flame
  Shall burn or purify them all.

'Tis true, it costs thee much of pain,
  And thou dost seem to suffer loss;
But wisdom bids thee not restrain
  The fire, that only burns the dross.

The golden ore, which thou hast cast
    In Love's consuming fire and strife,
Fears not the fiercest furnace blast,
    But brightens in its flames of life.

---

## LXII.

### THE DROP AND THE OCEAN.

Behold the vast, the sounding sea;
    And tell me, can its boundless flow,
Great emblem of eternity,
    A separation ever know,
    From the small drops that with it go.

Oh no! The drops and sea are one;
    And each from each existence take,
As to each other's arms they run;
    And all their thirst of being slake,
    In the great unity they make.

And thus with thee, oh feeble man!
    There is no reach, no power of art,
Which, variant from the heavenly plan,
    Can give thee strength or life, apart
    From life that flows in God's great heart.

Whate'er we call our own is Thine,
    Oh, life of God! oh living sea!
We live, and with a life divine,
    When our small drop flows into Thee,
    Made one in heavenly unity.

## LXIII.

### CHRIST THE WAY.

Just as I am, I take my stand,
With gates and bars on every hand;
And, with one act of faith and love,
Behold! the gates and bars remove,
And heaven comes brightly from above.

It was not done by books and creeds,
By tears, and prayers, and outward deeds;
I tried; but these could not control
The storms and tempests of the soul;
'Twas Christ, that came, and made me whole.

In Christ, who rules the stormy wave,
I found the arm with power to save;
He rent the gates and bars of sin;
He let celestial glory in,
And taught me God and heaven to win.

Oh sinning one! No more delay;
Christ is the true, the living way;
BELIEVE, and Christ's celestial art
Shall bid thy sins and fears depart,
And heal and save thy bleeding heart.

## LXIV.

### GOD'S INWARD TEACHING.

If thou wouldst have God's INWARD SPEECH
The centre of thy being reach,
And utter truths, that bear the sign,
And impress of a source divine;

*Take heed,* that all is free within
From pride and passion's noisy din,
Which turn away, and leave unheard
The whispers of the heavenly word.

'Tis when no angry billows roll,
And toss and agitate the soul;
'Tis in the calmness of the mind,
With pride subdued, and will resign'd;

That God's interior voice is near,
And faith bends low the listening ear,
And lessons high and pure are given,
Which breathe of peace, and truth, and heaven,

---

## LXV.

### GOD'S GLORY IN HIS SAINTS.

I thought, O God, Thyself to see,
   When I should reach the heavenly clime;
Display'd in kingly majesty,
   Upon a shining throne sublime.

But Thou didst say, Behold me *now*,
  Cloth'd in a vesture like thine own;
Mine eye illumes man's sainted brow,
  My love hath made his heart its throne.

In Christ the lesson first began;
  I dwelt in Him, and He in me;
And now each new-born, Christ-like man,
  Proclaims the same great mystery.

The holy man is God reveal'd;
  In HIM God makes *His glory known;*
Behold it, with thine eye unseal'd;
  BELIEVE! and make it *all thine own*.

---

## LXVI.

### THE CONQUEROR.

Wouldst thou the power possess
  All evil things to slay,
And, with the arm of victory,
  O'er life and death bear sway?

Wouldst thou go forth with strength,
  And with a force to tread
Upon the lion's fearful path,
  And crush the serpent's head?

Then gird thyself with LOVE;
  Put that bright armor on;
And know thine enemies shall fail;
  Thy victory is won.

  Like snow-flakes on the sea,
   That perish as they fall,
  They fade beneath LOVE'S mighty power,
   The CONQUEROR of all.

## LXVII.

### THE JOYS OF THE GOOD.

Let men of worldly power and arts
 The future love, the present hate;
It is the gift of holy hearts
 The bliss of heaven to ante-date.

While sighing worldlings oft exclaim,
 The hours are passing swift away;
To those of heavenly heart and name
 They circle round, but love to stay.

Our heart's emotions are as flowers,
 When cloth'd with pearls of morning dew;
With these we crown the passing hours,
 With chaplets bright and ever new.

Not night more surely comes to day,
 And day succeeds to starry night,
Than joys unnumber'd find their way
 To bosoms bath'd in heavenly light.

## LXVIII.

### LIVING BY THE MOMENT.

The morrow, when it comes, shall know
    Its daily task, its daily care;
But not till then it deigns to show
    Its needed act, its needed prayer.

Then to the PRESENT be thou true;
    To that let thought and act be given;
And thou shalt find a vigor new,
    To take the next great step to heaven.

Each moment's task and duty done,
    As ceaseless each to each succeeds;
Tis thus goes down life's setting sun,
    Serene and bright with worthy deeds.

'Tis thus, that heavenly bands shall greet
    Thine entrance to the realms of bliss;
Thy trials past, thy work complete,
    And crown'd with endless happiness.

---

## LXIX.

### FAITH IN GOD.

My faith, oh God, unshaken stands
In the great doings of Thy hands;
Thou hast the power, and Thou the will,
And what Thou sayest wilt fulfil.

I know the threatening, hostile host,
With many a proud, insulting boast,
Stands fiercely, in their banner'd wrath,
Across thy weeping children's path.

But faith looks up with tearful eye,
And prayer ascends with heart-felt cry;
And Thou, who see'st the mourner's tear,
And bending low, his prayer dost hear;

Thou, in the great appointed hour,
Thou, in the moment of Thy power,
Their banner'd host shalt smite and slay,
And sweep their impious strength away.

---

## LXX.

### DIVINE GUIDANCE.

Help me, Oh God, to run my race,
  Without a purpose of my own;—
To know no time, to know no place,
  But that which comes from Thee alone.

How vain and helpless every plan,
  Which builds itself on human choice;
The hope, the strength of feeble man
  Is found in listening to Thy voice.

Then let my roving thoughts be still,
  My earthly hopes and purpose slain;
And in their stead the glorious will
  Of God's great thoughts and purpose reign.

All thoughts, all hearts, oh God, control;
   And most of all, be this Thy care,
To build Thy kingdom in the soul,
   And wield Thy mighty sceptre there.

## LXXI.

### KEEPING TIME.

Whate'er our thoughts or purpose be,
   They cannot reach their destined end,
Unless, oh God, they go with Thee,
   And with *Thy* thoughts and purpose blend.

KEEP TIME WITH GOD, and then the power,
   Which in His mighty arm doth lie,
Shall crown the designated hour
   With wisdom, strength, and victory.

Be not too fast, be not too slow;
   Be not too early, not too late;
Go, where His orders bid thee go;
   Wait, when His orders bid thee wait.

KEEP TIME WITH GOD. Await His call;
   And step by step march boldly on;
And thus thou shalt not faint nor fall,
   And thus shalt wear the victor's crown.

## LXXII.

### THE DISTANT NEAR.

On earth we meet with friends and part;
And parting bear a sorrowed heart.
They come, they go; there's nothing sure;
All full of doubt; all insecure.

But when on earth our heaven we find
By having God within the mind;
The sorrow, which we felt before,
At parting friends, we feel no more.

However far our footsteps rove,
We always meet in God's great love;
However wide our travels run,
Our journey and our joys are one.

God is our home, and in that state
We cannot so far separate,
As not to make the distant near,
And know the lov'd are always here.

---

## LXXIII.

### DEATH OF THE ME.

In Christ's dear kingdom, 'tis not ME:
In Christ's dear kingdom, 'tis not THEE;
But ME and THEE, and MY and THINE,
Their separate life and power resign,
And clasp'd in ONE, become Divine.

The Me claims all things as its own;
And Thee and Thine make self their throne;
But in the soul that's born again,
The selfish Mine and Thine are slain,
And Universal Love doth reign.

Oh sacred unity of soul!
The separate parts in one made whole;
All strifes and jealousies unknown;
All partial interests overthrown;
God All in All, and God alone.

---

## LXXIV.

### GOD IN THE DARKNESS.

He sometimes walks behind the cloud;
And threatening storms His presence shroud;
His light is there; but all unseen,
Because the storm-cloud comes between.

From that dark cloud the bolts descend
The skies to cleave, the earth to rend;
But trusting hearts need not despair;
God guides the bolt; *our* God is there.

Oh transitory man and blind!
This consolation ever find;
That God, though shut from human view,
Is always present, always true.

As kind and faithful in the night,
As in the day-beam's cheerful light;
As kind and true, when storm-clouds hide,
As when the clouds are swept aside.

---

## LXXV.

### ANTICIPATIONS.

Departed ones, that shine afar,
  My earthly life is hasting through;
And soon, beyond the circling star,
  Shall wing its raptured way to you.

Oh come, and meet me in my flight,
  Oh come, and take me by the hand,
When first I greet celestial light,
  And tread the new, the heavenly land.

Long years have worn my furrow'd brow,
  And stained my cheek with many a tear;
But that is past, and brightly now
  I see the land of glory near.

Dear sharers of my joys and tears,
  Not dead, but only gone before!
Friends of my past, my early years,
  Oh, meet me on the shining shore.

## LXXVI.

### THE HOUR OF PRAYER.

It is the place and hour of prayer;
Oh, haste and meet together there.
Inspir'd with faith, relieved from care,
How sweet, how blest the hour of prayer!
    Sweet hour of prayer!

At that dear hour distrust retires;
The earth withdraws its vain desires;
And God, the Holy Ghost, inspires
The flame of heaven's celestial fires;
    Sweet hour of prayer!

'Tis then that truth shall guide thy ways;
'Tis then that prayer shall change to praise;
'Tis then that hearts and tongues shall raise
The song of heaven's unending days.
    Sweet hour of prayer!

---

## LXXVII.

### THE INWARD BURNING.

BE PATIENT, let the fire consume,
Give God's interior burning room.
Make no resistance, let it blaze,
And *self*, in root and branch, erase.

The life of self hath long annoyed;
Thy hopes assail'd, thy joys destroy'd;
It poisons every inward sense;
And FIRE alone can drive it thence.

The fiery trial gives distress;
But never wish its anguish less;
The pain thou feelest is a sign
Of flames from heaven, of fire divine.

Oh let it burn, till pride and lust,
And envy, creeping in the dust,
And wrong and crime, of every name,
Shall perish in the heavenly flame.

---

## LXXVIII.

### GOING HOME.

How pleasant 'tis, when life is run,
   And never more our steps shall roam,
To say with joy, our work is done,
   And we are GOING HOME.

How pleasant 'tis, our sorrows past,
   With better, brighter worlds in view,
To give one parting look, the last,
   And say with joy, ADIEU!

The sting of death hath lost its power
   To him who lives and never dies;
And death is the transition hour
   Which leads him to the skies.

Oh live, oh reign, departing one!
   Though gone from earth, to thee 'tis given,
With trials past, and victory won,
   To gain the life of heaven.

## LXXIX.

### THE FRUITS OF SUFFERING.

Oh let me suffer, till I know
   The good that cometh from the pain,
Like seeds beneath the wintry snow,
   That wake in flowers and golden grain.

Oh let me suffer, till I find
   What plants of sorrow can impart,
Some gift, some triumph of the mind,
   Some flower, some fruitage of the heart.

The hour of anguish passes by;
   But in the spirit there remains
The outgrowth of its agony,
   The compensation of its pains;

In meekness, which suspects no wrong,
   In patience, which endures control,
In faith, which makes the spirit strong,
   In peace and purity of soul.

## LXXX.

### GOD AND NOTHING.

We conquer ill and all distress,
By sinking into Nothingness;
For in our Nothing we are such,
That nothing can our Nothing touch.

Our enemies their arms prepare;
They smite, but find us empty air;
For when we see the lifted rod,
We leave ourselves, and hide in God.

We always know which way to run,
And thus all threatening dangers shun;
In vain they seek; they cannot find
Our hiding place in God's great Mind.

And when they undertake to smite,
They find that God is in the fight;
And God and Nothing make them know
A great and sudden overthrow.

---

## LXXXI.

### LOVE AND JUSTICE.

They tell us, we must first do right,
And not leave JUSTICE out of sight.
We answer, Look below, above;
And what is justice but to LOVE?

God's law is full of righteousness—
All truth, all justice; nothing less;
So just, it fills the world with awe;
And yet 'tis "*Love fulfils the law.*"

We LOVE, because we would be just;
We LOVE, because in God we trust;
We LOVE, because we would fulfil
His holy law, his holy will.

And he, who walks not in the light
Of Love, leaves justice out of sight:
Look where thou wilt, below, above,
And what is Justice but to LOVE?

---

## LXXXII.

### DIVINE PROTECTION.

Oh troubled soul, why thus complain?
Why thus great Providence arraign?
Poor, feeble heart! Thy troubles still,
And hide thyself in God's great will.

I know, it is thy trying hour;
Temptations throng with threatening power;
And many are the griefs that shroud
Thy pathway with their mid-night cloud.

But Jesus, dear and honored name,
Endured the toil, the cross, the shame;
And God, who guarded Him, shall be,
At last, the arm of strength to thee.

'Tis true, He now thy strength doth try,
Like birds that teach their young to fly;
But when thou sinkest, He will bring,
Beneath thy fall, his own great wing.

## LXXXIII.

### THE INWARD CHRIST.

The outward word is good and true,
But inward power alone makes new;
Not even Christ can cleanse from sin,
Until He comes and works within.

It was for this He could not stay,
But hasten'd up the starry way;
And keeps from outward sight apart,
That men may seek him in the heart.

CHRIST IN THE HEART! If absent there,
Thou canst not find Him anywhere;
CHRIST IN THE HEART! Oh friends, begin,
And build the throne of Christ within.

And know from this, that He is thine,
And that thy life is made divine,
When Holy Love shall have control,
And rule supremely in the soul,

## LXXXIV.

### FORGIVENESS.

Let men of hatred aim the blow,
    And point the cruel, jealous dart;
I will not fear, if I can know,
    The power of Love's forgiving art.

Oh God! Be Thou that living power;
    Make Thou my soul with pity strong;
That, in the sad and hostile hour,
    Forgiving love may conquer wrong.

They smite; but grant that in return
    My heart may seek to do them good;
And with its strongest impulse yearn
    To show its love and brotherhood.

In vain is all their angry strife,
    If God the mighty love hath given,
Which makes the soul's immortal life,
    And conquers hate with power from heaven.

---

## LXXXV.

### FOLLOW JESUS.

To follow Jesus is to be
    Possessor of His inward state;
His truth, His love, His purity,
    And all that made Him good and great.

To follow Jesus is to take
    The yoke of the great Father's will;
And friends and earthly good forsake,
    The Father's purpose to fulfil.

To follow Jesus is to go
    The bloody way of Calvary's cross,
If that can ward oppression's blow,
    And save humanity from loss.

Oh, be it ours to be like Him;
    Our thought, our purpose, and our prayer;
And thus the crown, that grows not dim,
    Of the great "Elder Brother" share.

## LXXXVI.

### NOT FORGOTTEN.

On the mountain He talked with Elias;
    On the mountain with Moses He stood;
They came from the heavenly mansions,
    From the home of the true and the good;

To utter dear words to sustain Him,
    In the terrible strife near at hand;
To proclaim, that no tomb should detain Him
    From the blissful and beautiful land.

'Tis the law and the hope of existence,
    The truth, which all ages declare;
That the good shall thus render assistance
    To the good, who have sorrows to bear.

And to thee, and to me, there are moments,
  In the days of temptation and sorrow,
When the sainted shall come with their message
  Of hope and of joy for to-morrow.

---

## LXXXVII.

### SUPREMACY OF LOVE.

Take to thyself celestial wings;
  Go, where thou pleasest, mighty LOVE;
In thee are life's eternal springs;
  Thou art the true, the heavenly Dove.

If there are hidden depths below,
  If heights and pinnacles in heaven;
The heavenly heights 'tis thine to know,
  To Thee the lowest depths are given.

If lines could bound Thee, life would die;
  If bars could hold Thee, heaven would cease;
For heaven doth live with Love's supply;
  And life goes out with Love's release.

Go, where Thou pleasest, heavenly Dove!
  And angels, from their thrones of light,
In depths below and heights above,
  Shall guard, but never bound thy flight.

## LXXXVIII.

### ENRICHED BY GIVING.

What blessedness it is to know,
We cannot feel for others' woe,
Without the added gift to heal
The griefs, which in ourselves we feel.

We cannot do the smallest thing,
With pureness in the offering,
Without repayment in the heart,
Far more than we ourselves impart.

Make of thy soul a ceaseless flood
Of pure, benevolential good,
A fountain, flowing out to men,
And heaven shall fill it up again.

Such is the heavenly way to live;
Whate'er thou hast, to others give.
GIVE LIFE TO OTHERS. Such alone
Know how to heal and save their own.

---

## LXXXIX.

### HOLY LOVE.

The love of self seeks earthly treasure,
   And close in secret chambers folds it;
But HOLY LOVE, no place, no measure,
   In all the universe can hold it.

Go, tread the path of secret fountains,
    And thou shalt find it shining bright;
Go, tread the forests and the mountains,
    And there it sheds its holy light.

Go, seek the poor man's cottage lowly;
    Ascend the monarch's lofty tower;
And, in the bosoms of the holy,
    'Tis everywhere their life and power.

It marches forth with banners flying;
    No sword can slay, no prisons bind it;
No fear, no grief, no pain, no dying,
    Can mar the happy souls that find it.

---

## XC.

### PERSEVERANCE OF LOVE.

Oh, be not weary, friend and brother;
    Oh, say not strength and heart are failing;
The proudest mark of Love and Lover
    Is this, that they are all prevailing.

The things, inspired by earthly forces,
    May stray in erring paths, and falter;
But Love, that runs in heavenly courses,
    Hath found the road it cannot alter.

There's nothing, if thou do but ask it,
    It is not ready in bestowing;
And nothing, if thy sorrow task it,
    Which finds not tears of pity flowing.

With strength subdued, and downward tending,
    The earth's ambition flags its pinion;
But Love, unwearied in ascending,
    Shall gain the height of heaven's dominion.

---

## XCI.

### LOVE AND THE ROD.

Oh, is it possible that God,
    If God is LOVE, men sometimes say,
Can frowning smite us with His rod,
    And seeming put His love away?

But know, 'tis Love's great evidence,
    Its proof, not always understood;
When, by its scourging outward sense,
    It builds the life of inward good.

Angry He seems, and sore doth smite;
    Strange thing for LOVE; and yet He knows
The mystic art, to bring delight
    From clouds, and storms, and heavy blows.

Oh LOVE! There's one thing pains the heart;
    The pang, when Thou art far away.
We cannot, cannot live apart;
    Smite, if Thou wilt, but only stay.

## XCII.

### REJOICING IN SORROW.

In the day of temptation and sorrow we sing,
    In the day of our grief we rejoice;
Because, in the storm-clouds their terrors that bring,
    We hear the storm-conqueror's voice.

Blow, blow, all ye winds from the north and the south,
    And storms from the east and the west;—
And yet as of old, by the word of his mouth,
    The stormy-tost wave is repressed.

When Christ walked in triumph on Galilee's lake,
    And hushed the wild tumult around;
'Twas a promise unfailing, He would not forsake
    His children, where'er they were found.

Blow, blow, all ye winds from the south and the north;
    The children ye never can harm.
When Christ, in the strength of His glory goes forth,
    He speaks, and the tumult is calm.

---

## XCIII.

### A PRAYER.

There is one thing my heart desires;
One thing its daily thought inspires;
Nor can my supplications rest,
Till this doth come, and make me blest.

'Tis Christ, not dwelling in the skies;
'Tis Christ, not seen with outward eyes;
But Christ, a principle within,
With power to purify from sin.

My longing aspirations claim,
More than an outward form or name;
A living power, a strength divine;
Oh, may that living Christ be mine.

Thy thought, Thy soul, Thine inmost heart,
Oh haste, and to my own impart;
In all Thy truth and glory come,
And make my soul Thy living home.

---

## XCIV.

### THE YOUNGER BROTHERHOOD.

Christ is the brother of the race;
  "The Elder Brother," it is true;
Come thou, and take the younger place,
  There is a brotherhood for you.

Oh, wonderful, redeeming plan,
  To make in all a Christlike heart;
And find another "Son of man"
  In all, who act the Christlike part.

Arise; the great design fulfil;
  Like Christ, go forth, and teach, and pray;
And seek to do the Father's will,
  In love and duty all the day.

And if the Eldest Son He came,
  With radiance from the realms above;
'Tis thine to bear the younger name,
  In the great family of love.

---

## XCV.

### A MORNING PRAYER.

Oh, Thou great Ruler of the sky,
  Who art, and cannot cease to be,
Whose power and greatness never die,
  We raise our Morning Prayer to Thee.

In the beginning of the day,
  With the bright rising of the sun,
Direct the footsteps of our way,
  Nor leave us till the day is done.

As hour succeeds to passing hour,
  And duties every moment fill,
Uphold us by Thy mighty power,
  And guide us by Thy heavenly will.

And thus, when all our days shall close,
  And suns no more for us shall shine,
Oh, may our souls in Thee repose,
  And life and joy be one with Thine.

## XCVI.

### THE SOUL AND THE SUN.

The night hath fled, the day begun,
   The earth resumes its smiling face;
And thus, with every rising sun,
   My soul lights up its daily race.

The clouds may intercept the rays,
   That from the sun's great centre shine;
But nought doth quench the central blaze;
   And nought shall quench the light that's mine.

And as the sun moves calmly on,
   His daily duty to fulfil;
So shall my life, in unison,
   Move onward in my Father's will.

No backward step, no long delay,
   No deviation's thoughtless maze;
For God Himself, with heavenly ray,
   Shall guide and guard in all its ways.

---

## XCVII.

### OH, DO NOT BLAME ME.

Had I a harp and tongue of gold,
Their powers could not the worth unfold,
The hidden depths, which LOVE conceals,
The sun-lit heights, which LOVE reveals.

There is no good beneath the sky,
If Love's dear life should fail and die;
There is no good, the skies above,
Without the jewell'd crown of Love.

OH, DO NOT BLAME ME, if I sing
The peace and joy, from Love that spring;
And cannot feel it cause of shame,
To sound the praise of Love's great name.

OH, DO NOT BLAME ME. 'Tis the heart,
Which makes, or mars, dear music's art;
And if sweet Love that heart shall fill,
How shall its singing life be still?

---

## XCVIII.

### LOVE'S REWARD.

The loving heart doth not regard
What selfish hearts would call reward;
And yet to acts of goodness true,
It always hath its work to do.

To private aims and objects blind,
It seeks the good of all mankind;
The only aim and work it knows,
Is that of healing others' woes.

It stands a wide and open door,
Where come the lame, the sick, the poor;
It heals the sick, the halt, the blind,
And calms the sad and troubled mind.

'Tis thus it lives for others' bliss,
  And its reward is only this;—
*The more its love to others flows,*
  *The more its power of loving grows.*

---

## XCIX.

### THE GOOD OF SORROWS.

'Tis painful thus to bear the Cross,
  To feel the long, the sorrowing hour;
But happy he, who finds his loss
  Made up in greater truth and power.

The tears we shed are not in vain;
  Nor worthless is the heavy strife;
If, like the buried seed of grain,
  They rise to renovated life.

It is through tears our spirits grow;
  'Tis in the tempest souls expand,
If it but teaches us to go
  To Him who holds it in His hand.

Oh, welcome, then, the stormy blast!
  Oh, welcome, then, the ocean's roar!
Ye only drive more sure and fast
  Our trembling bark to Heaven's bright shore.

## C.

### LEAVING THE PRISON.

Oh come, oh haste, imprisoned minds!
    Awake, to fatal slumber given!
'Tis LOVE that comes; our chains unbinds;
    He calls us up to life and heaven.

Love lights the prisoner's gloomy cell;
    LOVE rules the cottage; rules the throne;
He smites the tyrant's citadel,
    And everywhere He claims his own.

Old bards proclaim'd his mighty power,
    In earth's young days when time was new;
And now, in his triumphant hour,
    We find their prophet voices true.

Oh come, oh haste, imprison'd minds!
    Awake, to fatal slumber given!
'Tis LOVE that comes; our chains unbinds;
    He calls us up to life and heaven.

---

## CI.

### THE NOW.

Thou treadest with thy step sublime
The moment of the present time;
And he, who to Thy will would bow,
Oh God, must find Thee in the Now.

Oh, never shall our lives fulfil
The mandates of our Maker's will,
Unless with hearts of love and prayer,
And holy faith, we meet Thee there.

Oh grant us, then, with purpose true,
The strength our present work to do;
And crown, with all its needed grace,
The present time, the present place.

With step too fast, or step too slow,
We fail thy company to know;
And never to Thy will can bow,
Unless we find Thee in the Now.

---

## CII.

### UNITY OF HEARTS.

Thou art gone to the heavenly mountains;
  Thy lips breathe the heavenly air;
Thou art seated beside the bright fountains;
  And those, that thou loved'st, are there.

All heaven is glowing above thee;
  Around is the beautiful band,
Of the pure and the sainted, who love thee,
  Who live in the heavenly land.

Though lost to us here, we will bless thee,
  In thy flight to the mansions above;
Remembrance still lives to caress thee;
  Thou art still in the arms of our love.

Wherever thou goest, we find thee;
    Wherever thou dwellest, we dwell;
Our souls dare not linger behind thee;
    Our lips dare not utter FAREWELL.

---

## CIII.

### DYING TRIUMPHS.

The days of trial soon are o'er;
    Temptation, darkness, sorrow gone.
Already see the shining shore,
    And let the bark move swiftly on.

The waves are dashing round the prow;
    And hostile clouds are in the sky;
But wave nor cloud can hurt us now;
    Behold! The shining shore is nigh.

I hear them from the land of flowers;
    I see the bright, the happy band;
Row on! The victory is ours;
    We soon shall reach the happy land.

Row on! row on! 'Twill soon be o'er;
    And tears and toils shall be no more;
Let billows dash, let tempests roar;
    Our feet have touched the shining shore.

## CIV.

### LOOKING TO GOD.

Look to the heavenly Powers, to know,
    When earthly lights their aid refuse,
The path, in which thy feet should go,
    The path *to shun,* the path *to choose.*

Go not, when Selfishness invites,
    With instigation's wily art;
Urging to earthly, low delights,
    And scoffing purity of heart.

Go not, when Anger clouds the mind,
    However clamorous and strong;
Anger, the leader of the blind,
    The prompter to the false and wrong.

In faith, and love, and meekness call
    On Him, who knows thy weak estate;
And kindly hears and blesses all,
    Who patiently and humbly wait.

---

## CV.

### RECEIVING AND GIVING.

Flow on, Eternal waters, flow,
    Through the wide gate-ways of the soul;
Nor pause, nor intermission know;
    Coming and going, onward roll.

They bring a great, a healing power,
    But 'tis not brought to me alone;
I drink of their celestial dower,
    And, thankful, bid them hasten on.

ROLL ON TO OTHER HEARTS, and find
    The roots, which thou hast power to raise
In fruits and flowers, which make the mind
    A garden of celestial grace.

The heavenly life its greatness measures
    By heavenly goods to others given;
To keep from others' hearts its treasures
    Is shutting out itself from heaven.

---

## CVI.

### THE POWER OF FAITH.

I sat me down in earth's benighted vale,
And had no courage and no strength to rise;
Sad to the passing breeze I told my tale,
And bowed my head, and drained my weeping eyes.
But Faith came by, and took me by the hand;
And now the valley's rise, the mountains fall.
Welcome the stormy sea, the dangerous land!
With Faith to aid me, I can conquer all.
Faith lays her hand upon the lion's mane;
Faith fearless walks within the serpent's den;
Faith smiles amid her children round her slain;
When worlds are burning, cries unmoved, AMEN.
Yes, I am up, far upward on the wing;
The withered arm is strong, the broken heart doth sing.

## CVII.

### CHRISTIAN BENEVOLENCE.

Who is my BROTHER? 'Tis not merely he,
Who hung upon the same loved mother's breast;
But every one, whoever he may be,
On whom the image of a man's imprest.
True Christian sympathy was ne'er designed
To be shut up within a narrow bound;
But sweeps abroad, and in its search to find
Objects of mercy, goes the whole world round.
'Tis like the sun, rejoicing east and west,
Or beautiful rainbow, bright from south to north;
It has an angel's pinion, mounting forth
O'er rocks, and hills, and seas, to make men blest.
No matter what their color, name, or place,
It blesses all alike, the universal race.

---

## CVIII.

### LOVE THE SOUL'S DELIVERER.

The stormy clouds rolled o'er me,
    (I recollect it well,)
And heavily that darkness,
    Upon my spirit fell.
Upon my heart, and on my brow
Were griefs, which made that spirit bow.

But there was one above me,
　　Who saw my bleeding soul;
A strong, a true Deliverer,
　　Who came, and made me whole.
With skill surpassing human art,
He came, and nestled in my heart.

The tear, my cheek that sadden'd,
　　Ceased for myself to flow;
Because my heart was gladden'd
　　With healing others' woe.
'Twas LOVE with new-born hopes that came,
And kindled his celestial flame.

'Twas LOVE's sweet life that found me;
　　A Life not understood;
Which shed its joys around me,
　　In seeking others' good.
The sympathy, to others shown,
Return'd, and made its bliss my own.

---

### CIX.

#### PEACE AND INSPIRATION.

BE STILL! Let noise and passion cease;
　　Let heavenly quiet fill the mind
With gentle, pure, celestial peace,
　　To good and ill alike resign'd.

'Tis in the SILENCE of the soul,
    When peace invokes its mighty charm,
When passion's billows cease to roll,
    And all within is sweetly calm;

That INSPIRATION's power sublime,
    With truths before unknown, unheard,
Descends from heaven's angelic clime,
    Proclaiming heaven's eternal word.

'Tis then, that God, in whispers sweet,
    Comes near His lessons to impart;
And writes them in the Temple meet
    Of a resigned and quiet heart.

---

## CX.

### STAND STILL.

There is a time, when human pride
Will find it best to stand aside;
And let Almighty strength assume
The right of strife, the power of doom.

There is a time, when God alone,
With strength, to human arm unknown
Can bring the contest to a close,
With hope to friends, and fear to foes.

Fear not, that God will come too late;
In SILENCE learn; in PATIENCE wait;
He tries thy faith, but thou shalt see,
At last, His arm of victory.

At that dread hour, when man's weak will
Finds all its strength in STANDING STILL,
He comes with conquering arm and might,
And puts thine enemies to flight.

---

### CXI.

#### LIVING BY GIVING.

Whate'er we have, we GIVE;
    The Christ within the heart,
Through whom the heavenly life we live,
    Forever says, IMPART.

Christ's holy purpose is,
    The self-life to dethrone.
He is our Life; and all is His;
    We nothing call our own.

The man, who would retain
    What God in goodness sends,
Will find that he doth nothing gain,
    By low and selfish ends.

Give heart, and life, and all:
    Not any thing deny;
And, though thine earthly fortunes fall,
    Thy soul can never die.

## CXII.

### GOD'S TEMPLE.

Thy glory shines in flower and tree;
All nature hath its light from Thee;
Thy skill in all Thy works we sing,
Oh God, our maker, ruler, king.

But chiefly in man's form doth shine
A skill, a wisdom, more divine;
He stands erect; he walks confest
In strength and beauty o'er the rest.

That form, which holds immortal mind
For truth and goodness was design'd;
The TEMPLE, not of pride and strife,
Of God's divine, interior life.

Oh, keep it pure, that not a sin
With darkening stain may enter in;
And God, who knows and loves thee well,
Shall in that home of beauty dwell.

---

## CXIII.

### WORK TO-DAY.

The voice which claims the listening ear,
  Is that, which comes to thee TO-DAY;
Attentive lend thy heart to hear;
  Oh, turn not heedlessly away.

Thou knowest not to-morrow's sun;
  To-morrow's light is not thine own;
And what to-day is left undone,
  May ever be a thing unknown.

Whate'er it is, thou hast to do;
  Beneath whatever load to bow;
Be to thy sphere of duty true;
  Be up and doing.   Do it now.

## CXIV.

### SILENCE.

When, smitten, thou dost feel the rod,
BE STILL; and leave thy cause with God;
And SILENCE to thy soul shall teach
Far more than comes from outward speech.

When secret arts and open foe
Conspire thy peace to overthrow,
In silence learn the hidden power,
Which saves thee in that bitter hour.

Doth not thy Father take thy part?
Doth not He know thy bleeding heart?
And when it seems that thou wilt fall,
Doth not He feel it, bear it all?

MAKE NO REPLY.   But let thy mind
In silent faith the triumph find,
Which comes from injuries forgiven,
And trust in God, and strength in heaven.

## CXV.

### HAPPY CHRISTIANS.

I know a band, a happy band;
   I listen gladly while they sing;
Their dwelling is the blissful land,
   Where Christ is priest, where God is king.

They have no dark, repining days,
   But smiles and pleasures all the time;
Their thought is prayer, their prayer is praise;
   And prayer and praise make heaven's sweet clime.

Sometimes they dwell among the rocks;
   Sometimes they walk amid the storms;
But Faith defies the thunder-shocks,
   And turns the rock to heaven's bright forms.

Their heaven is NOW; their heaven is HERE;
   Celestial life to earth brought down;
Tis Faith, that fills their radiant sphere;
   'Tis Love illumes their sun-lit crown.

---

## CXVI.

### CHRIST'S FAITHFULNESS.

My soul will wait, till Thou return;
   Thou wilt not leave me here to die;
The love, that in thy heart doth burn,
   Is pledge enough, that Thou art nigh.

I cannot see Thee, but I know,
　That 'tis not far Thy footsteps rove;
My own dear love doth teach me so;
　There is no wandering in love.

I hear His footsteps, Oh, how soon
　His step, His voice, my heart doth cheer!
As at the sultry hour of noon
　His flock the shepherd's voice doth hear.

And thus my soul shall ever find,
　When tempters say, my LOVE doth roam,
A secret power within the mind,
　To call Him back, to win Him home.

## CXVII.

#### THE FIRST AND SECOND BIRTH.

When first we came upon the earth,
　We seem'd to know ourselves alone;
Within the bosom of that birth
　The love of *self* had built its throne.

For self we toil'd, for self we thought;
　'Twas self that rul'd without, within;
Till in its tyranny it taught,
　That life to self is life to sin.

Then with ourselves we came in strife;
　With help divine the foe subdued;
And substituted Inward Life,
　Which seeks the Universal Good.

With self cast out, and in its place,
    The reign of Universal Love,
'Tis easy now to run the race
    Of goodness here and bliss above.

---

## CXVIII.

### GOOD FOR EVIL.

When threatening clouds and tempests lower;
When foes exert their baleful power;
When many a false and cruel word,
From proud and hostile lips is heard;

To God look up. Make no reply;
On God's assisting grace rely;
Returning kindly acts and good
For all that's wrong, and fierce, and rude.

If thou canst thus thy kindness show
To those, who deal the hostile blow,
And that thy Spirit never shares
The cruelty, which dwells in their's,

Thy conquering soul shall victory win,
Against the battling hosts of sin,
And in its strength and virtue rise,
And claim a kindred with the skies.

## CXIX.

### THE DIVINE PATHWAY.

We have one choice, oh God!
    One path-way to pursue;
The way, which Jesus trod,
    Who came Thy will to do.

Whatever God commands,
    To do it or to shun;—
*That* is our work of heart and hands;
    *That* is our way to run.

No will we call our own,
    He gave us life and powers;—
'Tis *His* to make his pleasure known;
    To do that pleasure, *our's*.

And if the path be rough,
    And wounds our weary feet;
The way is God's, and that's enough,
    To make that roughness sweet.

---

## CXX.

### THE NEW TEMPLE.

Oh come, a Temple let us raise
To the celestial Maker's praise;
But built on the millenial plan,
A Temple in the heart of man.

A Temple, not of stone and wood,
A Temple, not of flesh and blood;
But fram'd of thoughts and pure desires,
And lighted up with holy fires.

'Twould be a work of folly, now,
To crown again Moriah's brow;
When that proud pile went down in gore,
It fell, to rise and shine no more.

But, in its stead, a House behold,
More glorious far than that of old;
A Temple of diviner art,
The Temple of a holy heart.

---

## CXXI.

### THE TRIALS OF LOVE.

Oft LOVE doth choose a toilsome road;
   And greatly thou dost fear His leading;
He places on thee such a load;
   Thy hands are lame; thy feet are bleeding.

He leads thee far to mountain heights,
   Or down in sunless depths descending;
He changes day to cloudy nights,
   With thunders and with flames impending.

On precipices takes His stand,
   Or walks on ocean's stormy water;
Or sudden shows a hostile band,
   Intent on threats, and blood, and slaughter.

But know the secret of His thought,
    In all these various ways TO TRY THEE;
And be, in all thy dangers taught,
    That LOVE, who tries, is EVER NIGH THEE.

---

## CXXII.

### THE JOYS OF SONG.

The bards poured forth their simple rhyme
In years far back, in olden time;
And strove to beat the sounding lyre,
Though more with earth's, than heavenly fire.

In all their states men love to sing;
Their heart-thoughts shake the vocal string.
They lov'd to sing in ages gone,
And still the song is marching on.

But louder rolls the sound to-day,
When those who sing have hearts to pray;
And prayer and praise in one unite,
In homage to the Infinite.

Awake the pleas'd, triumphant sound;
Let hearts to loving hearts rebound;
If ancient bards could sing so well,
Let our's a nobler anthem swell.

## CXXIII.

### HEAVENLY LIGHT.

The morning beams their light distil,
    And brightly glance on hill and mountain;
Their kindling blaze the forests fill,
    And clothe in beauty lake and fountain;
Dear emblems of the better day,
When sin and grief shall pass away.

'Tis thus their darkness to dispel,
    On weary hearts the light is breaking;
And all is right, and all is well,
    To souls with heavenly hopes awaking;
Who find the shadows of the night
Transform'd in morn's reviving light.

Depression plants the seed of hope,
    And greatness grows from humble station;
Of grief and tears we read the scope,
    As seen in heaven's illumination.
The gloomy grave, where nature dies,
Becomes the portal of the skies.

---

## CXXIV.

### FOLLOWING CHRIST.

Oh Thou, great Teacher from the skies,
    Who lived and died for men;
Teach us with Thee to sympathize,
    And be as Thou wast then.

It was the glory of thy heart,
    Whate'er Thou hadst, to give;
For others' sufferings to impart;
    For others' good to live.

Be Thou in us a living soul;
    Be Thou our spirit's power;
Its secret thought, its life's control,
    To guide it every hour.

We need like Thee a spirit true,
    A just and generous mind,
Which seeks, in all it hath to do,
    The good of all mankind.

## CXXV.

### GRATITUDE.

Oh God! With gratitude to Thee,
    'Our hearts go forth in holy song;
The gifts, which make us glad and free,
    To Thy beneficence belong.

Sweet consolations crown each day,
    With happy trust and heavenly peace;
They come with opening morning's ray,
    Nor with the setting sun-beams cease.

But humble hearts delight to know,
    That these abundant rich supplies
Can never from a fountain flow,
    Which hath its source below the skies.

To Thee, oh God, and Thee alone
    We owe the greatness of our bliss;
And gratefully our praise shall own
    The fountain of our happiness.

## CXXVI.

### CHANGE AND PERMANENCY.

The things of earth are always changing;
    And while we look,—all things are new;
Go forth; in all directions ranging;
    And changes ever meet thy view.

Each day, each hour, its life discloses,
    Transform'd alike in great and small;
But at the centre there reposes
    *One principle*, which binds them all.

The *form* of things is coming, going;
    The *life* of things doth always stay;
Love, at the centre, still bestowing
    A power, that knoweth no decay.

Motion and rest are thus together;
    And change and fixedness are one;
And, in our clouds and stormy weather,
    We always have a central sun.

## CXXVII.

### FAREWELL.

[Written on the death of a young friend, who, among other heavy sorrows, was afflicted with blindness.]

Farewell to Thee, daughter of sorrow;
   Farewell to Thee, maiden of grief;
At last the bright dawn of the morrow
   Hath brought to thine anguish relief.

No more, by the weakness that bound thee,
   Thy beauty and life are repress'd;
But, with radiance within and around thee,
   Thou art gone to the land of the bless'd.

Dear angel of light and of glory,
   Thine eye, that was clos'd here below,
With heaven's bright mansions before thee,
   Is open'd that heaven to know.

Farewell to thee, daughter of sorrow!
   The day-dawn hath welcomed thine eyes;
Thy night hath departed;—thy morrow
   Eternally bright in the skies.

---

## CXXVIII.

### OBEDIENCE.

Happy the man, who knows
   His Master to obey;
Whose life of care and labor flows,
   Where God points out the way.

He riseth to his task,
  Soon as the word is given;
Nor waits, nor doth a question ask,
  When orders come from heaven.

Nothing he calls his own;
  Nothing he hath to say;
His feet are shod for God alone,
  And God alone obey.

Give us, oh God, this mind,
  Which waits for Thy command,
And doth its highest pleasure find
  In Thy great word to stand.

## CXXIX.

### THE MULTITUDE OF SLAIN.

When the Millennium comes,
  Of love and peace the reign,
We all shall wondering look, and see
  The multitude of slain.

Stern pride, with sullen air,
  And hate, with scowling eye,
And troubled fear, and wild despair,
  Are destin'd all to die.

Suspicion's busy throng,
  And falsehood's lying breath,
And violence, and war, and wrong
  Shall sink to endless death.

Oh haste, MILLENNIAL day!
　　Bring back the brighter years;
And banish from the world its crimes,
　　And wipe away its tears.

---

## CXXX.

### CONTINUAL PRAYER.

The secret of continual prayer
　　Is this, *the prayer is always one.*
Discordant thoughts are never there;
　　It always says, "*Thy will be done.*"

All private purpose to forsake,
　　Accepting the Creator's plan;
Is of the Godlike to partake,
　　And realize the God in man.

God is the Universal Life;
　　God is the Universal Will;
'Tis our's to cease from nature's strife,
　　And in the Life of God be still.

Thus lost in Thee, we cannot cease
　　The everlasting prayer to raise;
Thus lost in Thee, our souls in peace
　　Become unchanging songs of praise.

## CXXXI.

### SIN AND SICKNESS.

Oh, when shall sickness and disease
Their persecuting warfare cease;
And weakness die, and grief and pain,
And death itself, at last be slain?

Doubt not, that better day is near,
The suffering sons of earth to cheer;
Disease and pain are born of sin;
Their remedy is found within.

Let Christ, descending from above,
Become incarnate in thy love;
And inward ills and wrongs subdue,
And make thy fallen nature new;

Let the great Healer make thee free
From sin's corroding malady;
And then the Life, that's in the soul,
Shall make the suffering body whole.

---

## CXXXII.

### CHRIST AND LOVE.

Wouldst thou the heavenly kingdom share,
Its fragrant flowers, its balmy air,
With bowers and blooms that never die?
Oh, then, look not beyond the sky,
BUT LOOK WITHIN, AND FIND IT NIGH.

That kingdom bright, without a shade,
That kingdom fair, of LOVE is made;
LOVE that is pure, and not asham'd,
That doeth good, and is not blam'd;
In Galilee the Christ 'twas nam'd.

Christ in the form hath pass'd away;
Christ in the *soul* knows no decay;—
But Christ thou dost not, canst not know,
In heaven above, or earth below,
If love within thee doth not glow,

Oh, who shall make thy spirit whole?
Who but the Love-Christ of the soul?
Worship at Love's celestial shrine,
And all that's heavenly and divine,
And good and true and fair is thine.

## CXXXIII.
### I SHALL YET PRAISE HIM.

At that dim hour, when ploughmen first arise,
Roused from their homely couch and deep repose,
When stars still linger in the changing skies,
And in the East the dawning feebly glows,
'Tis doubtful long, which of the two bears sway,
The nascent day or unextinguished night,
Till ruddy morn, at length, with bright array,
Proclaims the triumph of victorious Light.
So when there breaks upon the heart's domain
The Light Divine, which mars the shades within,
Oh, who can tell which of the two shall reign,
The recent purity or ancient sin?
And yet the inward Light, like outward day,
Shall shine, revealed at last, with a triumphant ray.

## CXXXIV.

### MEEKNESS OF SPIRIT.

When there are clouds and tempests in the mind,
And peace and mercy are by wrath displaced,
It breaks the plan of love which heaven designed,
And turns the blooming garden to a waste.
Then keep thy soul in peace and quietness,
And strive each evil passion to restrain,
And God will smile upon thee, and will bless,
And His bright image in thy breast maintain.
He, who did bow his blessed head in woe,
The Saviour of the meek and lowly heart,
Did He not pray for those who struck the blow,
And bless the ruffian hand that aimed the dart?
Oh, be like Him, calm, patient, self-controlled;
He, who can rule himself, has richer wealth than gold.

---

## CXXXV.

### FRUITS OF LOVE.

Love doth not seek the noisy feast,
   Which pampers earthly appetite;
Such pleasure is the last and least,
   That wakes its thought and gives delight.

In its own heart it finds its food;
   Cloth'd from within, and inward fed
By thoughts and purposes of good
   To others, needing clothes and bread.

Love doth not drain the sparkling bowl;
    Sings not the drunkard's song of woe;
It quaffs the wine-cup of the soul,
    The streams, from heavenly life that flow.

Forgetful of itself, 'tis bless'd,
    When it can calm another's fear,
When it can give the weary rest,
    When it can wipe the mourner's tear.

## CXXXVI.

### A PRAYER FOR LOVE.

Oh Love! Thy life is seen and heard
In kindly look, in gentle word;
A look, a word, that comes with power
In sorrow's dark and trying hour.

Oh, there's a sweetness in that tone,
A sweetness, born of love alone;
A magic in that gentle voice,
Which makes the broken heart rejoice.

Love utters no reproach severe;
Love wipes the penitential tear;
Love, with her gentle, soothing care,
Brings life and light to dark despair.

Oh, principle and life of Love,
That hast thy source in realms above,
Into our hearts benignant shine,
And make us, like thyself, divine.

## CXXXVII.

### RICHES OF LOVE.

Wouldst thou all knowledge have, and power,
    And riches scatter'd round thee bright;
Not only earth, but heaven thy dower,
    And all thy darkness chang'd to light;

With not a want, that's not supplied,
    And every day a day of rest;
With not a tear, that is not dried,
    And nought but sunshine in thy breast;

Oh, know the secret of this wealth;
    Go forth, the way of knowledge prove;
And outward strength and inward health
    Find in the heavenly art of LOVE.

'Tis LOVE, that maketh all things thine;
    'Tis LOVE, that bids thy griefs depart;
'Tis LOVE, that, with its power divine,
    Unites the world's divided heart.

---

## CXXXVIII.

### CHRIST IN THE SOUL.

If God is LOVE, and God and Christ are One,
Then Love becomes the Life-power of the Son;
And Love and Christ in essence are the same,
One central life, with difference of name:

And thus it is, when selfishness is dead,
And living Love is planted in its stead,
And doth the inmost faculties control,
That Christ is said to dwell within the soul:

CHRIST IN THE SOUL becomes the name and sign
Of inward life, eternal, and divine;
The life, descending from its home above,
The life of PURE AND UNIVERSAL LOVE.

---

## CXXXIX.

### LET GOD GUIDE.

Child of the truth, stand still,
    When clouds perplex thy view;
WAIT, till thy heavenly Father's will
    Shall teach thee what to do.

To go before the word
    Of God's command is given,
Can have no blessing from the Lord,
    No harmony with heaven.

Then wait for His command,
    Though long it may delay;
But when it comes, thy feet shall stand
    In heaven's appointed way.

If thus thy footsteps go,
    Where God hath made it plain,
Thy journey's end shall brightly show,
    Thou hast not gone in vain.

## CXL.

### LOVE THE FOOD OF THE SOUL.

The things, that, rightly used, would bless,
Are often evil in excess;
And just and innocent desire
Turns thus to passion's lustful fire.

And yet there is one TREE of joy,
Whose pleasant fruit shall never cloy;
The more we eat, the more there is
Of ever growing happiness.

The TREE, transplanted from above,
Which bears the fruit of heavenly LOVE;
Put forth thy hand, and taste, and live;
Not heaven itself hath more to give.

The children of celestial birth,
Who cannot live on things of earth,
Shall there the food and nurture know
From which immortal life doth grow.

---

## CXLI.

### LOVE AND HEAVEN.

I know that the heaven which thou teachest,
  Is a beautiful, beautiful place;
And that nought, with which art can enrich it,
  Could add a tint more to its grace.

How bright are the walls which surround it,
  With its gates and its towers ever new;
And numberless bloom the sweet flowers
  O'er the streams, that flow musical through.

But still 'tis no heaven for the spirit,
  If 'tis made but of music and flowers;—
The Heaven which the heart would inherit,
  Is a Heaven where Love builds its bowers.

The Heaven of the loving and living;
  Where the living all live in each other;
The Heaven of receiving and giving;
  Where each finds himself in his brother.

## CXLII.

### THE SOURCE OF HAPPINESS IN THE SOUL.

The soul hath power, through God's mysterious plan,
To mould anew and to assimilate
The outward incidents that wait on man,
And make them like his hidden, inward state.
If there's a storm within, then all things round,
The inward storm to clouds and darkness changes;
But inward light makes outward light abound,
And o'er external things in beauty ranges
If but the soul be right, submissive, pure,
It stamps whate'er takes place with peace and bliss;
If fierce, revengeful and unjust, 'tis sure
From outward things to draw unhappiness.
  Then watch, and chiefly watch, the inward part,
For all is right and well, if there's a holy heart.

## CXLIII.

### DIVINE TRUTH.

On every side mysterious things abound,
In earth and sky and ocean's deep domain,
Which man's poor reason utterly confound,
Beyond his power to fathom or explain.
His mind is dark. In what way shall he see?
Oh, God! Form Thou Thine image in my heart,
Implant Thy likeness in my spiritual part,
And help me to behold all things in Thee.
Thou art the source of light. That light, when through
My darkened mind its radiance is streaming,
In all its shadowy, secret places beaming,
At once dispels the dimness of my view.
In Thy light seeing light, my raptured eye
Doth everywhere behold love and infinity.

---

## CXLIV.

### THE CALMER OF THE STORM.

Oh Christ! I often think of Thee
Upon the waves of Galilee;
I hear the voice, I see the form,
Which rul'd the waves, which calm'd the storm.

That voice of power, which calm'd the seas,
Predicted "greater things than these;"
Those greater things to-day are seen
In this, that Thou dost RULE WITHIN.

To those who have the sight to see
There is an *inward* Galilee;
And it doth fit Thee now to bind
The waves and tempests of the mind.

Thou walkest now within the soul;
Thou bid'st its billows cease to roll;
The waves of stormy strife are still,
And pride and wrath obey Thy will.

---

## CXLV.

### REMEMBER THY CALLING.

Oh, leave them to their cruel words,
   Their words, that breathe of fire and slaughters;
And let us not forget, that we,
   Are LOVE's forgiving sons and daughters.

Our weapons all are form'd of LOVE;
   We know not, wield not, any other;
And he, who smites us, still doth bear
   The dear, the sacred name of brother.

For falsehood, truth; for evil, good;
   But never give thou scorn for scorning;
Thus hatred's brow of shades shall flee,
   Like night before the rosy morning.

And thus shall every evil fall,
   Forever from thy path departed,
And God shall be thine all in all,
   *If thou art only loving-hearted.*

## CXLVI.

### DIVINE STRENGTH.

Give us, oh God, the strength we need,
    Thy purpose to fulfil;
That we may show, in word and deed,
    A strong, unchanging will.

The war, in which our souls engage,
    Stands not with fickle hearts;
None but the strong that war can wage,
    With strength, which God imparts.

Oh, make us strong, and make us true,
    That we may not go back,
Though going on should lead us through
    The martyr's bloody track

Welcome the martyr's sanguine bed;
    Welcome his fiery crown;
Enough that Christ the way hath led;
    *Be our's to follow on.*

---

## CXLVII.

### THE SOUL'S NECESSITY.

OH, GIVE ME LOVE, or let me die;
    Oh, give me love, and all is well;
Such is my heart's continual cry;
    I ask no heaven; I fear no hell.

The more I know of love, the more
    Of God's celestial life I know;
'Tis something without bounds or shore;
    'Tis heaven above; 'tis heaven below.

Oh God, oh Love, oh heavenly Life,
    Celestial Truth, celestial Flame,
Burn up all selfishness and strife;
    Leave but THYSELF my soul to claim.

For hell doth perish in thy fire,
    And heaven comes down when love is given;
LOVE meets and fills my heart's desire;
    I know, I ask no other heaven.

## CXLVIII.

### FAITH IN TROUBLES.

The clouds are gathering in the sky;
With threatening wings the storm is nigh;
The sun himself doth hide his head,
As if his glorious light were dead.

And yet what means this inward calm,
With all things round in wild alarm;
This heavenly peace, which bids depart
All fear, all terror, from the heart?

'Tis this, that, in the threatening hour,
FAITH sees the great, controlling power
Of God's almighty presence near,
To guide and guard, to help and cheer.

Oh God, we know, a word of Thine
Can make the clouded sunlight shine;
We know the mandate of Thy will
Can make the stormy tempest still.

---

## CXLIX.

### FULFILMENT.

Oh Christ, 'tis our's with Thee to share
The sufferings which Thyself didst bear;
With Thee to toil, with Thee to bleed,
To help a suffering brother's need.

From youth's bright morn to manhood's day,
The cross upon His shoulders lay;
Until His sufferings found a close
In death for others' wants and woes.

His cross is on his followers still;
'Tis their's His sufferings to FULFIL;
And welcome each returning day,
With hands to toil and hearts to pray.

Oh sacred, sympathizing band!
In Christ's dear path and footsteps stand;
And what He did not live to do,
*Be that fulfill'd and done in you.*

## CL.

### MYSTERY OF THE NEW BIRTH.

I HEAR the mountain wind, but see it not;
Its mournful sigh startles my mind's repose;
I listen; but it passes quick as thought;
I know not whence it comes, nor where it goes.
'Tis thus with those, who of the Spirit are born;
A change comes o'er them; *how* they cannot say.
They wake, as from the darkness wakes the morn,
And mental night is changed to mental day.
'Tis God's mysterious work, 'Tis He can find,
Deep searching, and 'tis He can touch
The deep and hidden spring that rules the mind,
And change its tendencies, and make it such,
Redeemed, restored, as it was not before.
We know that 'tis God's work; but we can know no more.

---

## CLI.

### THE HEART SEARCHER.

If thou art ready in thy sin,
    CONVICTION'S deepest work to bear;
Then let LOVE'S mighty power come in,
    And search the hidden places there.

LOVE is the lamp that lights the mind;
    And he, who looks with love for light,
Shall never fail the place to find,
    Whate'er it is, of deepest night.

If wrongs thine inward life control,
    Ambition, pride, revenge, and lust,
Love is the Christ, who knows the whole,
    And brings to light the thing accurs'd.

Then shalt thou see it as it is,
    And learning its corrupting sway,
Shall smite the foe of truth and bliss,
    And drive him from thy heart away.

## CLII.

### A PRAYER FOR GUIDANCE.

Oh God, our GUIDE, our ONLY guide,
Watch o'er and keep us at Thy side;
And never let our footsteps stray
In error's wide and devious way.

However good our aims may be,
From pride and self, however free,
Not less our steps will miss the right,
If God shall fail to give us light.

And will He fail that light to send,
Unmindful of our fatal end?
Oh, will He fail to hear our cry,
And let us darkly grope and die?

It CANNOT BE. It will not be,
To those who wish that light to see;
To those, with earnest prayer who claim,
Amid the clouds, its guiding flame.

## CLIII.

### A PRAYER FOR HOLINESS.

Oh God, in this, our trying hour,
    With foes without, and foes within,
We need the Pentecostal power,
    Which smites and purifies from sin.

Oh, may that power, that breath divine,
    Consume, with its baptismal fire,
All in our souls that is not Thine,
    All worldly thought, all low desire.

Oh, may it put an end to strife,
    And pride and jealousy remove,
And crown us with the heavenly life
    Of truth, and purity, and love.

---

## CLIV.

### THE NEW BIRTH.

How foolish they, with thoughtless pride,
    And with the natural heart unslain,
Who set the words of God aside,
    Which say, THOU MUST BE BORN AGAIN;

Who sinfully and proudly think,
    'Tis vain on heavenly aid to call,
While standing closely on the brink,
    And ready soon to slide and fall.

Oh man, BE WISE; do not delay;
   Stay not upon the dangerous plain;
Haste to the mountain heights to-day,
   And be not number'd with the slain.

There is no safety for thy soul,
   No joy in heaven, no peace on earth,
Till Christ shall make thy spirit whole,
   *With heaven's renew'd, celestial birth.*

## CLV.

### UNITY OF LIFE.

There is a sacred bond which binds
In unity believing minds;
The dear, the blest, celestial tie,
Of those, *to selfishness who die.*

The bond, that cannot dwell alone,
The bond, that links to God's great throne,
And blends, like sunbeams with the sun,
God and His children, ALL IN ONE.

Division lines, that kept apart
The sacred unity of heart,
This new-born living power disclaims,
And smites, and throws them to the flames.

A power, with strength divinely given,
Which binds the hearts that once were riven;
And knowing neither great nor small,
Makes ALL OF ONE, AND ONE OF ALL.

## CLVI.

### GOOD FRUITS.

Cut down the tree that bears no fruit;
Destroy it, bud, and branch, and root;
It hath no claim, no right to live;
Its ashes to the tempest give.

Such is the great, the stern decree,
Which comes to all, which comes to me,
That all, who gifts and fruits deny,
Themselves shall be denied, and die.

'Tis this that makes the bliss of heaven;
It is for this that life is given;
That from our life the fruits may spring,
Which strength and life to others bring.

And he who fails in this great law,
Doth on himself the sentence draw,
Which smites the budless, fruitless tree
With death's unfailing destiny.

---

## CLVII.

### GOOD IN SUFFERING.

To mourn and fear, lest we may lose
    Some earthly good in earth's great strife,
Is but the trial to refuse,
    Which makes the nourishment of life.

Oh, rather let misfortunes fall;
    They cannot reach and harm the soul;
But only serve to disenthrall
    The inward life, and make it whole.

The greatness of thy suffering shows
    That God, who loves thee, *hates thy sin;*
And sends the message of His blows,
    To see if all is right within.

*Trust all with Him.* Affliction's stroke
    His work of mercy shall perform;
And leave thee, like the smitten oak,
    That's deeper rooted in the storm.

---

## CLVIII.

### 'TIS DONE.

'Tis done. No more my tempted heart
    In false and erring maze shall rove;
No more in thought and deed depart
    From the dear object of its love.

Such is my thought and purpose high,
    The fix'd design of heart and will.
Oh, thou great Ruler of the sky,
    Help me that purpose to fulfil.

Dear Strength and Majesty divine!
    Oh, listen to my heart's request;
Write on my soul, that Thou art mine,
    And with Thy favor make me BLEST.

## CLIX.

### LOOK TO JESUS.

Oh, thou weeping one and lonely,
   In thy bitterness of tears,
Look to Jesus, Jesus only,
   He will banish griefs and fears.

Worn with cares, and sad, and weary,
   All thy hopes and joys departed,
Oh, believe that He is near thee,
   Healer of the broken hearted.

With the day-light round thee closing,
   Nought but shadows on thy way,
On His heavenly arms reposing,
   Thou shalt find returning day.

Dare not trust to any other;
   Human help is all in vain;
But with love beyond a brother,
   Christ will give thee life again.

---

## CLX.

### THE POWER OF LOVE.

Go to the low, the base, the vile,
   The sinner and the publican;
And be thy only thought the while,
   *He is my brother man.*

Go to the weary, fainting heart,
    That only sinn d and wept before ;
And teach it the celestial art,
    To sin and weep no more.

Fear not. Doth not the sunbeam rest
    Upon corruption's festering tomb ;
And quicken from its dying breast
    The flower's celestial bloom ?

Go to the sinner in his sin,
    With love, the sunbeam of the skies,
And from the shades and death within
    Bid light and life arise.

## CLXI.

### FAITH.

Faith is the soul's interior sight ;
    And though the shadows hide the day,
Still, in the soul, the inward light
    Of Faith shall guide thee on thy way.

Ask, if thou wilt, of other lands ;
    Mount even to heaven's celestial sphere ;
Faith is the light of angel bands,
    The inward light, as it is here.

On secret errands oft they go ;
    God only hath the power to send ;
They do His will, nor seek to know
    The reasons, or the hidden end.

March on; and ever be content,
  Though shadows on thy pathway fall;
For this the light of Faith is sent,
  To cheer and guide thee through them all.

---

## CLXII.

### DEATH TO SELF AND LIFE IN GOD.

["But he, that is joined to the Lord, is one spirit." 1 Cor. vi. 17.]

Oh, sacred union with the Perfect Mind!
Transcendent bliss, which Thou alone canst give!
How blest are they, this pearl of price who find,
And dead to earth, have learnt in Thee to live.

Thus, in Thine arms of love, Oh God, I lie,
Lost, and forever lost, to all but Thee.
My happy soul, since it hath learnt to die,
Hath found new life in thine Infinity.

Oh, go, and learn this lesson of the Cross,
And tread the way, which saints and prophets trod,
Who, counting life, and self, and all things loss,
**Have found in inward death the life of God.**

## CXLIII.

### HE STANDETH AT THE DOOR.

The stars are shining from their depths of blue,
And one is standing at the door and knocks;
He knocks to enter in. His raven locks
Are heavy with the midnight's glittering dew.
He is our FRIEND, and great his griefs have been;
The thorns, the cross, the garden's deep distress,
Which He hath suffered for our happiness;
And shall we not arise, and let Him in?
All hail, thou chosen One, thou Source of bliss!
Come with Thy bleeding feet, thy wounded side;
Alas, for us, Thou hast endured all this;
Enter our doors, and at our hearth abide!
Chill are the midnight dews, the midnight air;
Come to our hearts and homes, and make Thy dwelling there.

---

## CLXIV.

### DIVINE PROTECTION.

Think not that the blest, whom the Lord hath befriended,
  Though scorned by the world, and though smitten with grief,
Will be left by the arm that has once been extended,
  To suffer and perish without its relief.

Oh, no! When the clouds of affliction and sorrow
  Encircle their souls with the darkness of night,
Thy mercy, oh God, like the sun of to-morrow,
  Shall gleam on the shadows and turn them to light.

He leaves us awhile to the billow's commotion,
  To see if our faith in the storm will remain;
But soon He looks out in his smiles, and the ocean·
  Is hushed from its threats, and is quiet again.

## CLXV.

### DESPISE NOT THE BEGINNINGS.

See, how beyond the hills, the morning bright
Doth write its coming with a single ray;
But gleam is joined to gleam, and light to light,
Till feeblest dawn expands to perfect day.
*Despise not the beginnings.* When the heart
Receives, however small, the primal beam
Which God doth to the new-born soul impart,
Revere and cherish its incipient gleam.
Though the first ray from Heaven's eternal throne,
The frail young shoot from Glory's morning star,
Yet fostered well, it dwelleth not alone,
But grows in its own light, and shineth far,
And bindeth ray with ray, till what was one,
Compacted of itself, expands a new-born sun.

## CLXVI.

### MEANING OF SORROWS.

'Tis well. I would not have it be,
  In aught, a change from what it is;
I have no hope, no joy but Thee;
  In Thee alone is all my bliss.

Oh God, oh Love, oh bliss Divine;
    To Thee whatever seemeth best;
Whate'er Thy will, that will is mine;
    The Cross from Thee is heavenly rest.

Thy blows are dear affection's arts,
    To win and bring me nearer home;
That home is in Thy Heart of hearts;
    I feel the rod; I cease to roam.

*Thine arm is round me.* Now I know
    The secret of the grief that press'd;
Thou would'st not, wilt not, let me go
    To other arms, to other rest.

---

## CLXVII.

### THE LIFE OF SELF.

The life which makes of Self its God,
    Thinks only of the ME and MINE;
Its fetter'd feet have never trod
    In the broad fields of THEE and THINE.

It bids its neighbor stand apart;
    It bears no brother near the throne;
But exiles from its prison'd heart
    All that it cannot call its own.

Arm of the Mighty! Rise and smite
    This stony wall, this prison gate;
Let in celestial truth and light,
    And LOVE's great empire re-instate.

Let every partial act and aim,
　And private hope and purpose fall;
Till all shall bear a brother's name,
　And God and Love be ALL IN ALL.

---

## CLXVIII.

### REJOICING IN GOD

The bird not always mounteth on the wing,
Nor doth he always his sweet music pour;
But as he silent on the branch doth swing,
He ever ready is to sing or soar.
The music, heard not, lingers on his tongue;
His flight is poising, ere it upward rise;
Thus shall his sudden harp of joy be strung,
And thou shalt see him mounting in the skies.
Oh, Christian, be it ever thus with thee,
When sitting here, thou with the earth dost blend;
Still as we mark thee, let us always see,
Thou hast a wing just poising to ascend,
And that the song, which hath no outward voice,
Still, in the inward soul, fails never to rejoice.

---

## CLXIX.

### THE SERVANT AND THE SON.

My life was once a life of care;
　I labor'd long; I labor'd hard;
And thought, that weary work should share,
　And nothing else, the great reward.

'Twas toil, when early morning broke;
    And toil, when clos'd the setting day;
At last a voice within me spoke;
    And told me, there's a BETTER WAY.

The servant's place, it said, resign,
    And take the birth-right of a SON;
And thou shalt know the bliss divine
    Of cares dispell'd, of labors done.

My troubled heart the message heard,
    And, while approving angels smil'd,
Received with joy the heavenly word,
    And found it good to be a CHILD.

---

## CLXX.

### PATIENCE.

She came, an angel cloth'd with light,
    Bright from the heavenly spheres;
And, coming, found me in the blight
    Of hopeless grief and fears.

Her name was PATIENCE. Calm her look,
    And gently kind her voice.
My trembling hand she gently took,
    And said, "My child, REJOICE."

There was such kindness in her air;
    Such love in all she said;
That soon the darkness of despair,
    The shades of sorrow, fled.

Dear angel of the better land,
  Bright from the shining shore!
Oh, ever hold me by the hand;
  Oh, *never leave me more.*

---

## CLXXI.

#### ALL SURRENDERED AND ALL GAINED.

WE GIVE UP ALL, oh God!
  Search us, our God, and see,
If in our hands there aught remains,
  Which is not brought to Thee.

All earthly goods we leave;
  Nothing we call our own.
Whate'er we hold, we hold it all,
  As Thine, and Thine alone.

And yet there is no loss,
  But rather heavenly gain;
It is the secret of the Cross,
  To gather good from pain.

In vain is earthly bliss;
  But there's a bliss divine,
A true, unchanging happiness,
  In this, THAT WE ARE THINE.

## CLXXII.

### THE WAY OF BLISS.

If thou wouldst know the way to bless
Thy soul with peace and happiness,
Then learn the path of him, who dies,
And makes *himself* a sacrifice;

The way, too little understood,
Which seeks its end in others' good,
Forgetting self, and giving all,
To aid, when want and suffering call;

The way of natures born again,
Of Christ alive, of Adam slain,
Which hath no thought, which hath no plan,
But that of good to suffering man;

This is the way, the royal way;
It never leads thy feet astray;
And he, who treads it, cannot miss
The great, *high road of happiness.*

---

## CLXXIII

### THE OUTWARD AND THE INWARD.

When Judah's Temple sank in flame,
  And hostile feet its ashes trod;
The human soul itself became
  The Temple of the living God.

From that great hour of blood and woes,
    The OUTWARD ceas'd; and in the heart
The INWARD in its beauty rose,
    Beyond the skill of outward art.

The living Temple is the SOUL,
    Renew'd enlighten'd from above;
With all its faculties made whole,
    And fill'd with purity and love.

Oh, turn from outward things WITHIN;
    Bow in the Temple of the mind;
Seek for a heart, that's free from sin,
    And God, and truth, and glory find,

## CLXXIV.

### FOLLOW GOD.

In that mysterious destiny,
    Which hath its plan in Heaven's great will,
There is a line of march for thee.
    Go bravely forth. Heaven's plan fulfil.

MARCH ON; nor falter in thy course;
    For He, the plan whose wisdom gave,
Will prove, in trial, thy resource,
    An arm of strength to guide and save.

TRUST NOT THYSELF. Thy strength is small.
    On human power do not depend;
There's one, who cannot fail or fall;
    His hand shall hold thee to the end.

Dark is the road; but o'er it shines
    A light from God, that grows not dim.
The keeper of his own designs,
    He knows the pathway. FOLLOW HIM.

---

## CLXXV.

### HOPE ON.

Remember, in thy griefs and fears,
    There comes a brighter hour than this;
And those to-day, who sow in tears,
    Shall find a harvest ripe with bliss.

Forget not, in thine hour of prayer,
    There's One, who hears thy voice of grief;
One, who will haste thy pains to share,
    And bring, in all thy woes, relief.

Then, be thy spirit undismay'd;
    HOPE ON, though all things seem to fail;
Till strength, in angel forms array'd,
    Shall o'er thy treacherous foes prevail.

Have Faith; and that shall surely be,
    For which thine earnest spirit cries;
With Faith thou shalt not fail to see
    The triumph o'er thine enemies.

## CLXXVI.

### CHRIST AND LOVE.

We live; but not a life of earth;
We live; but 'tis angelic birth;
   'Tis Christ that makes us whole;
But Christ below, and Christ above,
Where shall we find Him but in *love*.
   Love living in the soul.

"I live," the great Apostle said;
"And yet not I;" myself am dead.
   And yet 'twas not less true,
That, dead to self, he lived again
The life, that on the Cross was slain,
   The life forever new.

That Life was Christ, with Christ's great powers.
The Christ was his; the Christ is our's;
   The Christ in Love that's known,
Our earthly Life, like Paul's, is dead;
The Christ of love doth in its stead
   Erect his INWARD throne.

---

## CLXXVII.

### CELESTIAL VISITS.

Men, martyrs, priests of ancient time!
   Confessors of the early days!
Visit once more your native clime;
   Cloth'd bright with heaven's celestial rays.

In earth's forlorn and helpless state,
    We need the presence of the good;
The wisdom of the wise and great,
    To guide and bless our solitude.

Friends of the right, the good, the true,
    That wear at last the victor's crown,
Once more your earthly ties renew;
    Once more to earth's dim climes come down.

Open the portals of the skies,
    And from your realms of brightness there,
Console our sad and weeping eyes,
    And help our weary load to bear.

---

## CLXXVIII.

### HELP IN CHRIST.

'Tis true, the road we do not know,
And sometimes feel afraid to go;
But Christ, our Master, goes before,
*And where 'tis rough, will help us o'er.*

'Tis sometimes rocky, sometimes steep,
Or leads o'er foaming waters deep,
With cliffs, that frown above our head,
And snares beneath and pitfalls spread.

But, though it seems a dangerous way,
Let not our ready steps delay,
So long as Christ, our Leader, knows
The snares and dangers which oppose.

We do not know what's known to Him;
His eye is bright, though our's is dim;
To Him the way is straight and clear;
*Then let us follow without fear.*

---

## CLXXIX.

### PAST AFFLICTIONS.

'Tis good to cast a look awhile
   Upon the troubles of the past;
When heaven and earth, without a smile,
   With clouds and storms were overcast.

Dark was the day. To human sight
   There seem'd no hope, no power to save;
No favoring breeze, no guiding light,
   Nothing but sorrow and the grave.

But when inferior strength and skill
   The deadly blow could not withstand;
Our God, unseen, was with us still,
   His promise, and His favoring hand.

He seized the helm; His voice was heard
   Above the loud, tempestuous roar;
The stormy skies obey'd His word;
   Our bark in safety reached the shore.

## CLXXX.

### CONSOLATION.

The bitter tears, that thou dost shed,
    Fall fast to earth like vernal rain;
But, nurtur'd in their lowly bed,
    Shall rise in budding hopes again.

Weep on, if weeping is thy lot;
    Toil on, if toiling is thy share;
Thy toils and tears are ne'er forgot,
    If they are sanctified by prayer.

Such tears are never born to die;
    Like seeds beneath the vernal shower,
Instinct with immortality,
    They bloom again with fruit and flower.

From griefs shall heavenly joys arise;
    From toils celestial pleasures grow;
And if not sooner, in the skies,
    Thou shalt their heavenly meaning know.

---

## CLXXXI.

### MAN THE TEMPLE OF GOD.

Oh, where is God? Where shall my troubled mind,
The stamp and glory of the Godhead find?
Look forth, the wonders of creation scan,
And find that glory in the "*Son of Man.*"

Yes, in the humble Mary's infant child
The Godhead was revealed, look'd forth, and smil'd;
Not found in wood, or brass, or sculptur'd stone,
But in the human form, and there alone.

And wouldst thou now behold his glory shine,
Reveal'd in beauty and in grace divine,
Look on the renovated man, and see
The marks and brightness of the Deity.

Not man, obscur'd in *self*, and dead and lost,
But man, THE TEMPLE OF THE HOLY GHOST;
Man, in the spirit of the Christ made whole,
Pure in the outward life, and pure in souL

## CLXXXII.

### ONE THING LEFT.

Let envious men
My life and deeds defame,
And leave me nought but woe,
And burning shame.

Take from me all,
Of goods and home bereft;
So that the world shall say,
There's nothing left.

'Tis nought to me;
No inward thought complains,
If it can yet be said,
One thing remains.

Yes, all is well,
If He, who dwells above,
Shall fill my heart and life
With HOLY LOVE.

---

## CLXXXIII.

### THE SAFE PILOT.

Oh God! In my perplexity
   When dangerous doubts and fears prevail,
I love to look away to Thee,
   And ask Thee, how my bark shall sail.

Give Thou the winds, the currents Thou;
   May Thy great lights the path survey;
And thus my keel shall safely plough
   The terrors of the dangerous way.

SAIL ON. And banish doubt and fear;
   The hand the trembling helm controls,
Which doth the mighty mountains rear,
   And stormy ocean's billow rolls.

SAIL ON. 'Tis God that guides thee through;
   And, though thine eye is weak and dim,
There is one work thou still canst do,
   It is to LOOK AND TRUST IN HIM.

## CLXXXIV.

### GOD LOVED IN HIS CREATURES.

To LOVE THE LORD with all the heart,
 As it is understood by *Thee;*
What is it, Lord, but to impart
 *To all that live,* our sympathy?

Of every nation, name, and tribe,
 Thou art the life, the hope, the soul;
And wilt not, canst not, circumscribe,
 And love a part, and not the whole.

Of every thing on land and sea,
 Of things on earth and things in air;
There's none but hath its life from Thee;
 And none that doth not have Thy care.

In loving less than what Thou art,
 We love Thee with a love too small;
In Thee, the Universal Heart,
 We love the ONE, we love the ALL.

---

## CLXXXV.

### CHRIST REVEALED THROUGH HIS FOLLOWERS.

  If thou wouldst have the world to prize,
   And of the wonders tell;
  The glory and the mysteries,
   That in the Saviour dwell;

Then put thyself the Saviour on,
    And clothe thee with His light,
Nor let the dress, thou oft hast worn,
    Exclude Him from their sight.

Oh, Christian, what a shame it is,
    That thou thy sins dost bear,
When raiment, made of righteousness,
    It is thy right to wear.

Oh, let that holy garment shine,
    That all around may see,
And magnify the Lord divine,
    Whose brightness beams from thee.

## CLXXXVI.

### THROW OFF WORLDLINESS.

Man's spirit hath an upward look,
    And robes itself with heavenly wings;
E'en when 'tis here compelled to brook
    Confinement to terrestrial things.

Its eye is fastened on the skies;
    Its wings for flight are opened wide;
Why doth it hesitate to rise?
    And still upon the earth abide?

And would'st thou seek the cause to know,
    And never more its course repress;
Then from those wings their burden throw,
    *And set them free from worldliness.*

Shake off the earthly cares that stay
    Their energy and upward flight;
And thou shalt see them make their way
    To joy, and liberty, and light.

---

## CLXXXVII.

### THE SECRET SIGN.

They know Him by the *secret sign,*
    Which to their souls is given;
'Tis written there in light divine,
    With characters from heaven.

They may not tell it; but 'tis there,
    Forever deep impressed.
Nor grief, nor pain, nor sharp despair,
    Shall rend it from their breast.

The child the parent's accent knows,
    The accents ever dear;
Unlike the treacherous voice of foes,
    That fills his heart with fear.

He runs to meet it; and it falls
    In blessings and in joys;
And thus, whene'er the Saviour calls,
    His people know his voice.

They know him by the *secret sign,*
    Which to their souls is given;
'Tis written there in light divine,
    With characters from heaven.

## CLXXXVIII.

### JOY IN GOD.

Although affliction smites my heart,
    And earthly pleasures flee,
There is one bliss that ne'er shall part,
    My joy, oh God, in Thee.

That joy is like the orb of day
    When clouds its track pursue;
The shades and darkness throng its way;
    But sunlight struggles through.

O Thou, my everlasting light,
    On whom my hopes rely;
With Thee the darkest path is bright,
    And fears and sorrows die.

---

## CLXXXIX.

### TRIUMPH IN DEATH.

On earth when the journey allotted us closes,
    When the hour and the moment of parting are near,
If a gleam, on that parting, of mercy reposes,
    Oh, wish not, oh think not, to fasten us here.

"Tis true, there is strength in the ties which endear us,
    And bind us so closely to things here below;
But bright is the land, where no sin can come near us,
    And bliss is disturb'd by no moments of woe.

Then joy to the soul, that is ripe for ascending,
   And breathe not a sigh that shall tempt it to stay,
When angels in triumph its flight are attending,
   And Bethlehem's star is the light of its way.

---

## CXC.

### REMEMBRANCE IN PRAYER.

When at the hour of prayer thy heart
The fervor of its love discovers,
In secret as thou kneel'st apart,
And many an angel round thee hovers,
    Oh, then remember me!

When down thy cheek the tear-drops roll,
Of gratitude for sins forgiven,
And thou dost feel within thy soul
A ray of joy just sent from heaven,
    Oh, then remember me!

For who, that sees thee trembling, kneeling,
Or may thy meek entreaties hear,
To Heaven so fervently appealing,
Will not believe that God is near?
    Oh, then remember me!

Ask not for earthly pomp, or pleasure;
A humble, meek, and holy heart
To me is far a greater treasure
Than earth's vain glories can impart.
    *Oh, thus remember me!*

## CXCI.

### THE UNIVERSAL MAN.

Oh Christ! I thank Thee for the book
    Thou writest in thy Life divine;
The mirror, where I love to look,
    That I may make Thine image mine.

That image stands before me bright,
    Surpassing human skill and art;
Oh, that its pure, celestial light
    May come to me, and fill my heart.

Thou wast not Jew; Thou wast not Greek;
    No sect, no party, marr'd Thy plan;
Thou cam'st Thy brother man to seek;
    Thyself, the UNIVERSAL MAN.

Thou askest not his place or name,
    His earthly ill, or earthly good;
Enough to Thee, the sacred claim
    Of MAN alone, of BROTHERHOOD.

---

## CXCII.

### WAITING IN FAITH.

Oh wait! The time will come at last.
Oh wait! The storm will soon be past.
Already, in thy quicken'd view,
Behold the sunlight breaking through.

Canst thou rebuke and calm that storm
And mould its clouds to beauty's form?
Canst thou, with human skill, defy
The thunder's voice, that shakes the sky?

Oh no! Thou only hast' the power,
To stand and know the fearful hour;
And in its strength and terrors see
The signs of heavenly majesty.

Then WAIT; in humble calmness WAIT;
Till peace its reign shall reinstate;
The tempests sweep the troubled air,
But Christ controls them; God is there.

## CXCIII.

### THE BATTLE GOING ON.

'Twas said in days of ancient time,
  When men of faith in Judah stood,
And with prophetic words sublime,
  The wicked warn'd, and cheer'd the good:

That men of heavenly love and fear,
  Of truth and faith, of works and prayer,
Should find conflicting forces near,
  And bloody persecutions bear.

And now, as in the days of old,
  The prophecy of strife is true,
And blows, and tears, and griefs untold,
  Shall follow close the faithful few.

Yes! it shall be, as it hath been,
  And coming years the strife shall see;
The good shall strive, and striving win,
  But win through tears and agony.

---

## CXCIV.

[It is sometimes thought, that the devotedness and holiness of heart, which is expressed by "Christ in the soul," is not favorable to the discharge of outward and active duties. So far from this being the case, the truth is, that the performance of such duties faithfully and lovingly is the natural and necessary result of inward holiness.]

### SOMETHING TO DO.

In idleness is danger lurking;
  Arise, and put thy sickle in;
The day is calling for thy working,
  The ripened sheaves and harvests win.

The sun to run his race is rising;
  Then be thou ready for his light;
The deed and plan of good devising,
  With all thy hand, with all thy might.

Say, is there not some one in sorrow,
  Some fainting head, some bleeding heart;
Trust not the doubtful, unknown morrow;
  To-day thy pitying aid impart.

The suffering world for aid is sighing;
  And little is it understood,
That he himself is lost and dying,
  Who hath not life in doing good.

## CXCV.

[" Christ in the Soul" is sometimes a sorrowful spirit. Jesus wept. And those, who bear His spirit, are not without tears. The following lines were written, when, in crossing the Atlantic some years since, I passed near the spot, where one of my adopted sons lost his life by shipwreck. And I may say further, they were written under a sudden and remarkable impression of his apparently restored and real presence with me during some hours. An experience so remarkable that it affected me much, and left a lasting impression.]

### LINES FROM THE OCEAN, ON A SON LOST AT SEA.

Boy of my earlier days and hopes! Once more,
   Dear child of memory, of love, and tears!
I see thy crush'd and faded life restore
   The stamp and brightness of its opening years.

The same in youthful look, the same in form,
   The same the gentle voice I used to hear,
Though many a year hath pass'd, and many a storm
   Hath dashed its foam around thy cruel bier.

Deep in the stormy ocean's hidden cave,
   Buried and lost to human care and sight,
What power hath interposed to rend thy grave?
   What arm hath brought thee thus to light and life?

I weep,—the tears my aged cheek that stain,
   The throbs once more that swell my aching breast,
Embody years of anxious thought and pain,
   That wept and watched around that place of rest.

Oh, leave me not, my child! Or, if it be,
   That, coming thus, thou canst not longer stay,
Yet shall this kindly visit's mystery
   Give rise to hopes, that never can decay.

Dear, cherished image from thy stormy bed!
   Child of my early woe and early joy!
'Tis thus at last the sea shall yield its dead,
   And give again my lov'd, my buried boy.

---

## CXCVI.

[Lines, written in February of 1853, on visiting the temples and tombs in the mountains of Thebes in upper Egypt.]

### CHRIST THE SOURCE OF IMMORTAL LIFE.

The oar is dipping in the waves,
   That bear me on their watery wings.
Farewell to Egypt's land of graves!
   Farewell, the monuments of kings!
They died;—and chang'd the living throne
For chambers of the mountain stone.

I trod the vast sepulchral halls,
   Designed their lifeless dust to keep,
And read upon the chisell'd walls
   The emblems of their final sleep;
And learned, that when they bow'd to die,
They hoped for immortality.

Dark was the way.  They knew not how
    That other life would come again,
To rend the flinty mountain's brow,
    That overlooks the Theban plain.
But if aright their hearts they read,
The rocks at last would yield their dead.

Oh yes!  The instincts of the heart,
    In every land, in every clime,
The great, ennobling truth impart,
    That life has empire over time.
Death for eternal life makes room,
And heaven is born upon the tomb.

They saw the end, *but not the way*,
    The life to come, but not the power;
And felt, when call'd in dust to lay,
    The doubt and anguish of the hour.
Oh Christ!  By Thee the word is spoken;
The power is giv'n; the tomb is broken.

---

## CXCVII.

[One day, when travelling in the waste and barren peninsula of Sinai, I observed a small flower,—a very uncommon object there,—springing up by the lonely pathway, which gave rise to the following:]

### THE FLOWER OF THE DESERT.

One day in the desert
    With pleasure I spied
A flower in its beauty
    Looking up at my side.

And I said, Oh sweet flow'ret,
    That bloomest alone,
What's the worth of thy beauty,
    Thus shining unknown?

But the flower gave me answer,
    With a smile quite divine;
'Tis the nature, Oh, stranger,
    Of beauty to shine.
Take all I can give thee,
    And when thou art gone,
The light that is in me,
    Will keep shining on.

And, Oh, gentle stranger,
    Permit me to say,
To keep up thy spirits
    Along this lone way,
While thy heart shall flow **outward**
    To gladden and bless,
The fount at its centre
    Will never grow less.

I was struck with its answer,
    And left it to glow
To the clear sky above it,
    And the pale sands below;
Above and around it
    Its light to impart,
But never exhausting
    The fount at its heart.

## CXCVIII.

[One of the marked results of that deep spiritual experience, which constitutes the inward Christ-life, is a tender and sympathizing feeling for the animal creation. The absence of such feelings is a discouraging and even fatal sign. I once knew a little girl, whose kindness had succeeded in taming the fishes and even the turtles in the small lake, near which she resided. I have myself witnessed her beautiful control over them; and seen her collect them in great numbers, and feed them from her hand.]

### THE MAIDEN FISH-TAMER.

Oh maiden of the woods and wave,
   With footsteps in the morning dew !
From oozy bed and watery cave,
   The tenants of the lake who drew.
Thy voice of love the mystery knew,
Which makes old bards and prophets true.

They tell us of that better day,
   When love shall rule the world again ;
When crime and fraud shall pass away,
   And beast and bird shall dwell with men ;
When seas shall marry with the land,
And fishes kiss a maiden's hand.

The iron age has done its best
   With trump and sword and warriors slain ;
But could not tame the eagle's nest,
   Nor lead the lion by the mane ;
With all its strength and all its woe,
There was an art it did not know.

'Twas fitting that a maid like thee,
  In childhood's bright and happy hour,
Should teach the world the mystery
  That youthful innocence has power;
That love the victory can gain,
Which is not won by millions slain.

Oh man, if thou wouldst know the art
  The shatter'd world to reinstate,
Like her put on a loving heart,
  And throw away thy guile and hate.
A maid shall tell thee how 'tis done,
A child shall show the victory won.

---

### CXCIX.

[Lines, expressive of religious experience, and written, when travelling at night in 1853, in the wilderness of Mount Sinai.]

### THE STAR THAT SHINES UPON THE HEART.

I marked the bright, the silver star,
  That nightly deck'd our desert way,
As shining from its depths afar,
  Its heavenly radiance seem'd to say;
Oh look! From mists and shadows clear,
My cheering light is always here.

I saw thee. And at once I knew,
  Star of the desert, in my heart;—
That thou didst shine, the emblem true
  Of that bright star, whose beams impart,
From night to night, from day to day,
The solace of their inward ray.

There is a beam to light the mind;
  There is a star the soul to cheer;
And they that heavenly light who find,
  Shall always see it burning clear;
The same its bright, celestial face,
In every change of time and place.

Star of my heart, that long hast shone,
  To cheer the inward spirit's sky!
Illumin'd from the heavenly throne,
  Thou hast a ray that cannot die.
*'Tis God that lights thee.* And with Him
No sky is dark; no star is dim.

## CC.

[Written, on reaching the city of Jerusalem, after having visited other prominent places in Palestine.]

### THE SACRED LAND.

Oh land of men of other days!
  Where bards and ancient prophets trod.
The land of rapt Isaiah's lays,
The land of David's psalms of praise,
  Land of the men of God.

And if 'tis not enough of fame,
  To be the home of prophets,—then,
From all thy hills and rocks proclaim
The higher and more glorious name
  Of *Him who died for men.*

In vain, like birds on ocean's foam
    When tossed amid a troubled sea,
In vain the sad in spirit roam,
In search of resting-place or home,
    Who turn away from thee.

By thee the seal of doubt is broken,
    Which long to human hearts had pressed;
By thee alone the words are spoken,
Which "peace on earth" and love betoken,
    And give the weary rest.

The clouds of Sinai's mount proclaim
    The law that wakes the spirit's fears;
From Calvary's height the message came,
The law of love for that of flame,
    Love for the coming years.

Land of the soul! forever dear;
    Wide o'er the world the words impart,
Which turn to hope despairing fear;
Which dry the penitential tear,
    And heal the bleeding heart.

---

## CCI.

[Written on visiting the vast, silent sands of the Lybian desert, which bound the valley of the Nile.]

### GOD WITH US IN SOLITUDE.

'Tis thus in solitude I roam
    O'er many a land and tossing sea;
And yet, afar from friends and home,
    I find, O God! a home in Thee.

I pass from things of space and time,
    The finite meets or leaves my sight;
But God expands o'er every clime,
    The clothing of the Infinite.

He left me not in that far land,
    Which I have lov'd to call my own;
And walking now on Egypt's sand,
    I feel that I am not alone.

He walks the earth, He rides the air;
    The lightning's speed He leaves behind
His name is LOVE. And tell me,—Where
    Is sea or land He cannot find.

Oh long I've known him. Could it be,
    That, if He did not hold me dear,
He thus would travel land and sea,
    And throw His arms around me here?

I could not leave Him, if I would;
    I would not, if the power were given;
'Twould be to leave the True and Good,
    The soul's Repose, the spirit's Heaven.

## CCII.

[The following records the impressions, left upon the mind, on visiting the garden of Gethsemane, May, 1853.]

### THE VICTORY OF THE CROSS.

Oh let me not forget! 'Twas here,
   Earth of the Saviour's grief and toil!
He knelt;—and oft the falling tear
   Mingled his sorrows with thy soil,—
When, in the Garden's fearful hour,
He felt the great temptation's power.

Here was the proffer'd bitter cup.
   "THY WILL BE DONE," The Saviour said.
His faith received, and drank it up;
   Amazed, the baffled tempter fled,—
Repulsed, with all his hate and skill,
Before an acquiescent will.

Oh man! In memory of that hour
   Let rising murmurs be repress'd;
And learn the secret of thy power
   Within a calm and patient breast.
"THY WILL BE DONE." 'Tis that, which rolls,
Their agony from suffering souls.

Such is the lesson that I find,
   Here, in the Saviour's place of tears;—
The lesson, that the trusting mind
   Has strength to conquer griefs and fears;
And doom'd upon the cross to die,
Finds death itself a victory.

## CCIII.

[The following, which I have translated from one of the poems of Madame Guyon, was written during her long imprisonment in the state prisons of France. It strikingly illustrates the resignation and triumph of a soul, wholly given up to the will of God.]

### RESIGNATION AND TRIUMPH IN AFFLICTION.

A little bird I am,
   Shut from the fields of air;
And in my cage I sit and sing
   To Him, who placed me there;
Well pleased a prisoner to be,
Because, my God, it pleases Thee.

Nought have I else to do;
   I sing the whole day long;
And He, whom most I love to please,
   Doth listen to my song;
He caught and bound my wandering wing,
But still He bends to hear me sing.

Thou hast an ear to hear;
   A heart to love and bless;
And, though my notes were e'er so rude,
   Thou wouldst not hear the less;
Because Thou knowest, as they fall,
That love, sweet love, inspires them all.

My cage confines me round;
   Abroad I cannot fly;
But, though my wing is closely bound,
   My heart's at liberty.
My prison walls cannot control
The flight, the freedom of the soul.

Oh, it is good to soar,
  These bolts and bars above,
To Him, whose purpose I adore;
  Whose Providence I love;
And in Thy mighty will to find
The joy, the freedom of the mind.

---

## CCIV.

#### THE TRUE REST.

'Tis not in vain the mind,
  By many a tempest driven,
Shall seek a resting place to find,
  A calm like that of heaven.

The weak one and dismayed,
  Scarce knowing where to flee,
How happy when he finds the aid,
  That comes alone from Thee.

In Thee, oh God, is REST;—
  Rest from the world's desires,
From pride that agitates the breast,
  From passion's angry fires.

In Thee is rest from fear,
  That brings its strange alarm,
And sorrow, with its rising tear,
  Thou hast the power to calm.

## CCV.

### GOD THE SOURCE OF LOVE.

O Thou, who giv'st the true desire,
    THYSELF the only source of love,
Within our humble hearts inspire
    Affections, springing from above.

As transient as the morning dew,
    Earth's love imparts its joys in vain,
But those, who drink the fountain true,
    The dews of life, thirst not again.

Why then should men with watchful eye
    The treasure seek which is not given?
The cisterns of the earth are dry,
    Perennial flow the draughts of heaven.

O Thou, who giv'st the true desire,
    THYSELF the only source of love,
Within our humble hearts inspire
    Affections, springing from above.

---

## CCVI.

### RESOURCE IN TEMPTATION

My Saviour! Wilt Thou leave me now,
    When sharp temptations round me throng?
All other helps have failed—and Thou
    Alone canst hope and truth prolong.

TEMPTED;—but can I turn away,
  And give my thoughts to aught but Thee;
Oh, let me die; but ne'er betray
  My pledge of truth and constancy.

I know that sorrow has its power,
  I know that pleasure has its charm;
But oft the least propitious hour
  Beholds the triumph of Thine arm.

Oh, who or what shall lead to sin,
  Whate'er its power, whate'er its art—
So long as Christ is King within,
  And binds His being round my heart?

---

## CCVII.

### SORROW THE NURSE OF LOVE.

Oh God, Thou heard'st my early vow,
('Twas sacred then, 'tis sacred now,)
The vow which promised to fulfil,
With Thee to aid me, all thy will.

Resigning all the soul held dear,
It pledged Thee, with a heart sincere,
Never, oh, never, to incline
To plan or choice, which was not Thine.

And Thou hast put me to the test
In times and ways Thou thoughtest best;
But He, who smote me, gave the power
To conquer in the trying hour.

When sickness Thou didst on me send,
When Thou didst take each dearest friend;
I found, in spoiling earthly bliss,
Thou mad'st *Thyself* my happiness.

My earthly loss, my earthly pain,
Was changed to joy and heavenly gain;
And Thou didst grieve me but to prove,
*That sorrow is the nurse of love.*

---

## CCVIII.

### GOD'S FAITHFULNESS.

I know, Oh God, that dangers near
    Are thick on every side;
But Thou hast taught me not to fear,
    With thy dear hand to guide.

What altered purpose, what decay,
    What turning from the right,
To God's great heart can find its way,
    And change the Infinite?

If earth's affections treacherous prove,
    If earthly bonds are riven,
There still remains a higher love,
    Unchangeable as heaven.

The sun his shining way may leave,
    The ocean leave the shore;
The sun no more the day to give,
    The sea to heave no more.

But Thou, more lasting than the sea,
   More certain than the sun,
Canst break no bonds of unity,
   *When hearts with Thee are one.*

---

## CCIX.

### QUIETNESS OF SPIRIT REFLECTED IN THE LIFE.

When from the heart its ills are driven,
   And God, restored, resumes control,
The outward life becomes a heaven,
   As bright as that within the soul.

Where once was pride, and stern disdain,
   And acts expressing fierce desire;
The eye, that closest looks, in vain
   Shall seek the trace of nature's fire.

No flame of earth, no passion now,
   Has left its scorching mark behind;
But lip, and cheek, and radiant brow,
   Reflect the brightness of the mind.

For where should be the signs of sin,
   When sin itself has left the breast;
When God alone is Lord within,
   And perfect faith gives perfect rest.

## CCX.

### THE MYSTIC DOVE.

["And John bare record, saying, I saw the Spirit descending from heaven like a *dove*, and it abode upon him."—JOHN 1: 32.]

The mystic Dove has found its nest ;
    Its snowy wings are folded there ;
Within the pure, the peaceful breast,
    Where faith and praise are joined to prayer.

Long did the weary wanderer roam ;
    But scared from scenes of strife and fear,
It's panting bosom found a home,
    In hearts to truth and virtue dear.

And if it took thee long to find,
    Oh, haste not from thy home to stir ; —
But nestling in the holy mind,
    Cease not to be its comforter.

The soul that claims thee, bright with love,
    Is beautiful as thine own skies ;—
Fear not, dear stranger from above,
    Fly not, sweet bird of Paradise.

www.ingramcontent.com/pod-product-compliance
Lightning Source LLC
Chambersburg PA
CBHW032158160426
43197CB00008B/970